ARGENTINA IN COLLAPSE?

THE AMERICAS DEBATE

MICHAEL COHEN · MARGARITA GUTMAN

(EDITORS)

ARGENTINA IN COLLAPSE?

THE AMERICAS DEBATE

New School University
The New School

INSTITUTO INTERNACIONAL
DE MEDIO AMBIENTE Y DESARROLLO
AMÉRICA LATINA

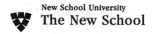

New School University

The New School

66 West 12th Street
New York, NY 10011

This book is sponsored by the New School University
and is published with the support of the Ford Foundation.

1st edition: December 2002
© of the 1st edition: Instituto Internacional de Medio Ambiente y
Desarrollo, IIED-América Latina

Editor: Margarita Pierini
Design: Mariana Nemitz
Proofreading: Nicolás Meyer

ISBN: 987-98033-2-9
Printed in Argentina
Deposit made as established by law 11,723

Cover illustration:
New and most exact map of America. Described by N. I. Vischer, enlarged and
corrected according to L. Bleau and others.

Acknowledgements

This book would not have been possible without the intellectual and programmatic support of The Ford Foundation. Jorge Balán recognized the importance of an interdisciplinary conference addressing the recent socio-political upheaval in Argentina, and helped make it happen in a matter of months. It is with his help that The New School's Graduate Program in International Affairs was able to hold the conference, "Economic Management and Political Collapse in Argentina: Interpreting the Past to Build for the Future," in New York in April 2002. Manuel Montes provided valuable suggestions on participants and the substantive design of the conference. The release of the Spanish edition of this book, in August 2002, was made possible by Augusto Varas, The Ford Foundation's Representative for the Andean Region and Southern Cone, in Chile.

The contents of this book are based on the substantive contribution of the authors: Tulio Halperín Donghi, Roberto Frenkel, Nicolás Dujovne, José Marcio Camargo, Andrés Solimano, Néstor García Canclini, Adriana Clemente, Ernesto Semán, Berardo Dujovne, Joseph S. Tulchin, Joseph Stiglitz and Jeffrey Madrick. Several others made significant contributions as conference participants: Jorge Balán,

Adhemar Bianchi, Torcuato Di Tella, Caroline Moser, Victoria Murillo, Lance Taylor, Diana Tussie, and Augusto Varas.

We would also like to recognize the institutional support of The New School, led by its President Bob Kerrey and Dean Ann-Louise Shapiro. Logistical support was provided by a persistent team: Chong-Lim Lee, conference coordinator, Lexanne Hamilton, Kristi Allen, George Calderaro, and Pam Tillis.

This book was produced with intense editorial work from Margarita Pierini in Buenos Aires and Chong-Lim Lee and Ernesto Semán in New York, with graphic design work from Mariana Nemitz. To all of them, we express our gratitude for their efforts to meet the tight production schedule and editing process of this volume.

The intellectual challenges of understanding and interpreting the socio-political events that have shaken Argentina from an interdisciplinary approach are enormously complex. We are thus grateful, lastly, to the fruitful intellectual collaboration that has contributed toward this volume. We hope it serves as a modest contribution to the understanding of the past and the present, with the aim of building a more sustainable, socially just, and equitable future. As a small step toward joining theory with action, proceeds from the sale of *Argentina in Collapse? The Americas Debate* will be donated to Caritas Argentina, for its work to improve childhood nutrition.

Michael Cohen • Margarita Gutman
Buenos Aires - New York
September 2002

TABLE OF CONTENTS

INTRODUCTION

MICHAEL COHEN

MARGARITA GUTMAN

On December 20, 2001, the four-year recession in Argentina culminated with the resignation of President de la Rúa, following political demonstrations, police violence, and the deaths of 29 people. De la Rúa's resignation not only pointed to Argentina's dire economic situation, but presaged the country's political collapse as well, with four persons holding the presidency in under two weeks. The second president, Adolfo Rodríguez Saá, declared the country in default on its $150 billion external debt, making Argentina the largest defaulter in history.

By Christmas 2001, 15 million people or 40 percent of the population had fallen below the poverty line. Mass social and political mobilizations erupted, with Argentines voicing their anger in numerous *cacerolazos*, or street demonstrations, which had been unseen since the mid-1980s. On the evening of January 10, 2002 alone, these demonstrations occurred in 50 locations throughout Buenos Aires. The *cacerolazos* reflect the interests of many groups, not only the middle class; some of the graffiti found after the *cacerolazos* in December 2001 were signed, "The People."

During the 1990s, many described Argentina as the "poster child" or "favorite student" of the international financial institutions. The country followed a set of macroeconomic policies including trade liberalization, deregulation, privatization of public services, and strict monetary policy. Sustained economic growth through the first half of the 1990s appeared to some, including the official institutions, to confirm the wisdom of those policies. Others, however, warned of increasing indebtedness, rising unemployment, and growing inequality and poverty. Academic analysts noted that the so-called benefits of external liberalization and privatization had not materialized. While these effects are deeply troubling within Argentina, they are also of great significance in Latin America and the developing world more generally. If Argentina had followed the "best advice" of the global institutions, what had gone wrong?

The new government of Argentina, led by President Eduardo Duhalde, has redirected macroeconomic policy, breaking sharply with the past and questioning the validity of the International Monetary Fund's policy recommendations. The Argentine experience has also provided new insights about the real options available to countries in economic and political crises in an age of globalization. Meanwhile, popular rejection in Argentina of politicians from all parties reflects the perception that the country's collapsing economy is not just the result of misguided policies from the external world, but rather the responsibility of Argentine politicians and national institutions as well. The events in Argentina mark a watershed in the current global debate about the role of both national and international institutions in development policies and economic management of developing countries.

In order to understand this difficult period and its implications beyond Argentina and the present, this volume brings together a selection of the papers from an international conference, "Economic Management and Political Collapse in Argentina: Interpreting the Past to Build for the Future," organized by The New School's Graduate Program in International Affairs with the support of the Ford Foundation, and held in New York City on April 8 and 9, 2002.

This book examines Argentina's recent economic and political collapse from perspectives that are both interdisciplinary and transcontinental. Its contributors bring the diversity of their views as historians, economists, sociologists, journalists, and architects from Argentina, the United States, Chile, Mexico, and Brazil. The dramatic events that have unfolded in Argentina over the past year are analyzed from the historical perspective of the last century, with a special focus on the 1990s, aiming to identify lessons for the future and contribute to the search for sustainable development. The Argentine case is important for Latin American countries and the whole world. Nobel Laureate Joseph Stiglitz highlights its importance in Part V, where he denounces the convergence between national mismanagement of economic policies, in the face of the pressures of the global economy, and the erroneous advice of international institutions.

Opening the book, eminent Argentine historian Tulio Halperín Donghi considers why Argentina adopted its particular form of the neoliberal model. In Part II, Argentine economists Roberto Frenkel and Nicolás Dujovne, and noted economists from MERCOSUR, José Marcio Camargo from Brazil and Andrés Solimano from Chile, evaluate Argentina's decade of convertibility in the 1990s. Part III builds on the economists' understanding of the crisis with a diversity of other perspectives: Néstor García Canclini explores the new spaces of expression opened within culture; Adriana Clemente looks at the social dimensions of the crisis and its impact on poverty; Ernesto Semán identifies issues key to understanding the political crisis; and Berardo Dujovne analyzes the urban impact of the crisis. In Part IV, Joseph Tulchin reflects on the close linkage between convertibility and Argentina's relationship with the United States. In Part V, Nobel Laureate Joseph Stiglitz cites the lessons Argentina offers for Latin American development. Looking ahead, in Part VI, Michael Cohen suggests issues to be included in a development agenda and Margarita Gutman uses concepts of ideology and utopia to examine the choices made in the 1990s and alternatives for the future. The book includes an epilogue by Jeffrey Madrick on the origins of neoliberalism and its impact in Argentina.

The papers included in this volume and the presentations made at the conference triggered intense debate among the New York audience, which included many Argentines and Latin Americans. Many of them agreed on convertibility's negative impact on the economy, as an ideology adopted by successive governments to justify a *statu quo* that in fact benefited few and excluded many. Further, the doctrinaire faith in this ideology – that the peso remain pegged to the dollar lest catastrophe and hyperinflation befall the economy – impeded exploration of economic alternatives. Conference participants considered the degree to which this ideology blinded governments, officials, and the media, precluding wider public discussions on alternatives for Argentina's future. They also deliberated on the question of responsibility at the national and international levels. Closing the two-day conference, Professor Stiglitz's comments reinforced these conclusions, pointing to the IMF's unsound economic advice, based on neither evidence nor experience, and Argentina's culpability in taking up this advice. He thus echoed the findings that emerged over the course of the conference, of the responsibility of both national and international actors for the events culminating in the December 2001 collapse.

I

Background to the Crisis

1

WHY DID ARGENTINA ADOPT A NEOLIBERAL MODEL?

TULIO HALPERÍN DONGHI

Historians are always wary of answering questions that start with *why*; they know how difficult it usually is to find a persuasive single answer to them. In the case of Argentina, however, the problem is perhaps the opposite. In 1991, neoliberalism appeared to be the obvious choice. It would have appeared obvious even if Argentina had not been forced to adopt such policies in its search for foreign credit and investment to overcome its second bout of hyperinflation in two years, without imposing an unbearable social burden on a population notorious for reacting with extreme outrage to economic adversity.

The question will be then not *why* but *how*; namely, *how* did Argentina reach a point where an instant conversion to neoliberalism offered the only way out from a desperate economic situation? In exploring this question, I am very aware of historians' convictions of the imperative of examining the entire history of the country in question. I will try to avoid this pitfall by highlighting the particularly relevant features of Argentine's past.

Argentina's past has had a reversal of fortune more dramatic than that of most other countries. During the "long century" that started with the opening of the River Plate region to world trade by the last Spanish Viceroy in 1809, to the 1929 breakdown of the world trade system, the country experienced one of the highest rates of economic growth in the world. Its integration into the expanding North Atlantic economy appeared to be a marriage made in heaven and blessed by the Invisible Hand. There was universal agreement on this point. Even José Hernández, whose *Martín Fierro* is usually described as a denunciation of the social costs of such a road to progress, found nothing essentially wrong with Argentina becoming "the pastoral colony of Europe," because Europe was becoming "the industrial colony of Argentina."

The consequences of this long period of almost uncontrollable growth were manifold. Perhaps the first was that Argentina forged a new economic and social core in the lowlands of the littoral and pampas provinces by attracting overseas immigrants in a higher proportion to nationals than any other "new country." The conventional date for the start of the mass immigration process is 1870, but already in 1869, more than three-quarters of the male inhabitants from ages 16 to 60 were foreign-born in the nation's capital. This almost indigestible foreign mass was to be assimilated with minimal fuss and at such a speed that the process was completed before the assumption that Argentina would forever be a land of increasing prosperity, began to be disproved. While there is no doubt that this assumption was part of the reason for the intensely patriotic feelings of the new Argentines, perhaps it later became the reason why even adversities much less extreme than the current one evoke existential doubts about the country's ability to survive.

Another consequence was that despite efforts to create a solid institutional and political framework for the country, these results always emerged more slowly than the frantic rate of growth. By the early twentieth century, power was vested in a political class based in the most archaic sections of Argentina. Even so, general prosperity allowed it to rule against surprisingly little opposition. In 1912, when electoral law effected universal franchise, which had been on the books for almost a century, it was not the result of social pressure but a miscalculation by the country's rulers of the populace's indifference to politics as deference toward them.

In four years, the political elite found themselves out of power and the turbulent social change that followed was deeply resented by its victims in the traditional political class. Once in power, the Radical party, having built an unbeatable political and electoral machine, proved unable to understand, let alone cope with, the new challenges brought by the post-1929 depression. Conservative forces led the agitation that brought about the first break in institutional continuity since the opening of the constitutional era in 1862.

Starting in the 1930s, Argentina experienced a half century of perpetual political crises that were punctuated by military takeovers: first, the relatively enlightened, pseudo-democratic Conservative regime, which retained power through systematic electoral falsification; then, an authoritarian regime of plebiscitarian democracy that, under Perón's leadership, won the lasting support of the popular classes; followed by two attempts at restoring electoral democracy while denying power to the Peronist party, still the largest in the country then, which unsurprisingly ended in failure. This opened the way for a triumphant return to power of the Peronists, who became immediately entangled in an increasingly bloody war between their left and right, and were replaced in turn by a military regime that attempted to solve the crisis once and for all through state terror. Finally, in 1983, the country fell back into democracy, almost by default.

Half a century of political instability could not but have consequences on all walks of national life. Perhaps the most insidious of these was the increasing inability of the government, whose authority was ephemeral and insecure, to maintain even a semblance of control over public administration performance. The decadence of the state began in earnest in 1955, after the fall of the first Peronist regime, when the lifespan of regimes in power went from more than ten years to two to three years. While the consequences were felt everywhere, none was more important than the state's increasing inability to call upon the taxes it notionally raised. It was this inability, rather than excessive public expenditures, that encouraged governments to avoid bankruptcy by resorting to high inflation and later to foreign borrowing for much longer than prudent.

The chronic malaise created by the equally chronic political crisis combined with memories of pre-1929 prosperity created a universal conviction that Argentina's economic performance was much worse than it actually was. (In fact, between 1932 and 1947, the country enjoyed fifteen years of swift recovery followed by impressive growth. Between 1963 and 1975, it underwent a more modest, but still quite respectable, expansion. In the 1960s, however, nobody took seriously Gino Germani's opinion that Argentina did not have a serious problem, and that her only problem was that she did not know this.) Besides contributing to the despondent mood of the country, this pessimistic assessment encouraged governments to repeatedly attempt crash programs in search of economic recovery.

These programs, however, were each dropped as soon as it appeared that their overly ambitious goals would not be achieved as quickly as had been hoped. Such a pattern thus extended to economic policies the fitful rhythm that characterized Argentine politics. Not surprisingly, this repeated experience strengthened the conviction that speculation is less risky than long-term investment, making the success of each new economic program even more unlikely than that of the previous one.

If we look beneath this constantly agitated surface, an underlying trend is recognizable, guiding the seemingly chaotic succession of events that led Argentina to seek shelter in neoliberalism. The starting point of this trend was the second invasion of the political arena by an improvised mass movement that gave total control of the state to Peronism in 1946, a current that a few months previously did not even exist.

Peronism has never ceased to puzzle foreign observers for its obvious ideological incongruences and its ability to retain the support of successive coalitions of similarly incongruous partners. Nevertheless, beneath these idiosyncrasies, its profile as a party was essentially determined by the context of its birth, in which the rising economic tide that brought Argentina out of the depression was reaching its highest level, bringing about a dramatic expansion of the industrial working class. The growth of the industrial sector had been stimulated first by the drastic fall in Argentina's ability to import due to the depression and later by her almost complete isolation from her overseas industrial goods suppliers because of the war. There were reasons to fear that local industry would not survive the shock of an even limited return of industrial imports. To put Peronism's predicament in a nutshell: in a society whose industrial sector was supported by the flimsiest economic foundations, it was born as a movement that sociologically

— albeit neither ideologically nor organizationally — was close to the British Labour Party, and similarly had its backbone in the labor movement.

After Peronism lost power in 1955, it became clear that its predicament was also that Argentine society had acquired a new shape and was determined to retain it. As Perón had become aware years before his fall, this reshaped society could not survive by simply maintaining the stranglehold, through government fiats, on the external sector that originated during the depression and war. Any opening threatened to modify a balance of social forces that enjoyed the support of a very wide consensus.

The persistence of this dilemma contributed to the political stalemate that characterized the eighteen-year interregnum between the fall and then restoration of Peronism. That, in turn, brought about an unacknowledged interim solution: the advances in the wage earners' share of national income were allowed slowly to erode while full employment was substantially maintained. Because the economy continued to grow, real wages did not fall with the wage earners' declining share of national income. Perhaps more importantly, since stability depended on the unions' ability to counteract the erosion of real wages caused by inflation, the labor movement was ensured a more influential role than when Peronism had been in power.

What made the situation even more attractive to organized labor was that its clout within the marginalized but still powerful Peronist movement was further enhanced by its enervated political branch. By using its social as well as its political clout, organized labor managed not only to protect the legal framework introduced by Peronism, and thus its monolithic structure, but used the opportunities offered by periods of increased political instability to extract further concessions from weak governments. It created first a vast network of tourism hotels and a few years later, an even more impressive system of hospitals and health care centers sustained by its members' mandatory contributions.

A trend was beginning to emerge, that is only now running its full course. The interim solution to the Peronist dilemmas avoided a frontal attack on the social profile that developed under it. It also produced a slow but unrelenting hollowing of that profile, hidden by the strengthened institutional framework that represented constantly weakening social forces. The metalworkers union, which had become the largest labor organization by 1955, offered the most extreme example of this trend. While its membership shrank with the ongoing crisis in the myriad of midget enterprises that had flourished in a totally closed economy, its influence over the labor movement and over Peronism at large grew. Its rise reached such a point that the metalworkers union's leader fashioned himself as a rival of Perón for the leadership of the movement that bore the exile's name.

This trend continued even through the terrorist state that followed the brief and disastrous second Peronist administration. While the military rulers partially honored their proclaimed commitment to neoliberal principles, they were also determined to avoid any significant rise in unemployment. While expanding the already large sector of state-owned enterprises, for a time they could achieve all these contradictory goals because of the availability of exceptionally cheap foreign credit in exceptionally large amounts. As these circumstance changed, it paved the way for the succession of events that was to culminate in the military rulers' hasty abandonment of power. The military rulers' erratic economic performance had shown that they were closer than they were aware to the consensus of those that cherished the memories of the good old Peronist times.

Raúl Alfonsín, elected in 1983 as the first president of the resurrected Argentine democracy, was also the first to defeat Peronism in an entirely free election, but totally aware of his allegiance to the social legacy of the Peronist revolution. Alfonsín sought to integrate this legacy as a central dimension of an effective and fully democratic political culture. He faced economic obstacles in the process, which he preferred to ignore until it proved too late. The outcome was a devastating bout of hyperinflation that finally convinced Argentines that the society that emerged from an ephemeral post-war prosperity was dead beyond any hope of resurrection. After having consumed all of the nation's reserves in the vain effort to perpetuate for decades the short-lived conjuncture of 1945-48, they were finally forced to admit defeat.

The effort to protect the society that emerged in the early post-war years had introduced enough incremental changes to make it possible for an alternative social profile to emerge from the ruins of Peronist Argentina. While President Alfonsín continued to place the relation between the state and organized labor at the core of the "social question," his most important social program, in fact, was the *Plan Alimentario Nacional*, which distributed basic foodstuffs to needy families. Already in 1983, the Argentine working class was losing its central place among the popular sectors, which were well advanced in their refashioning into the poor who would always be among us.

Peronism was left to guide Argentina into a post-industrial era eerily reminiscent of the pre-industrial one, and this is less surprising than one would imagine. If the movement has retained more vitality than its hopelessly decadent former backbone, it is because it has maintained a dual link with the popular sectors since its birth. This duality is symbolized by the two mythical roles assigned to Eva

Perón, as the militant "standard-bearer of the workers" and as the "Lady of Hope" for the downtrodden. Today, as shantytowns invade the rust belt on the outskirts of Buenos Aires, a remnant of the recent industrial past, one finds refugees of urban and rural unemployment gathering by the hundreds of thousands. Hilda González de Duhalde can legitimately invoke the example of Eva Perón as the inspiration for a patronage machine that selectively covers the basic needs of the old and new urban dwellers of Buenos Aires.

After discovering that it will never become the replica of a Western European country that its founding fathers had promised to root in the deserted plains of the pampas, Argentina was ready to remodel itself on the example of a Central American republic. Argentina has a vast mass of the poor living hand to mouth, a shrinking middle class whose most fortunate members can afford vacations in Orlando's Disney World, and a very small, very rich group that gravitates around a political leadership that has much in common with the "kleptocracies" of Eastern Europe. As we have all just learned, however, it was to fail in its attempt to become a Western European country.

II

Assessing a Decade of Convertibility:
Four Latin American Perspectives

2
BENEFITS AND COSTS
OF CONVERTIBILITY

ROBERTO FRENKEL

MACROECONOMIC PERFORMANCE,
EMPLOYMENT AND INCOME DISTRIBUTION[1]

On December 1, 2001, Domingo Cavallo, then Minister of Economy, announced among other measures, the decision to establish controls and restrictions on transactions on the foreign-exchange market. He thereby put an official end to the monetary regime that he himself had launched slightly more than ten years before. An economic breakdown and wave of social turmoil and political turbulence brought President De la Rúa's administration to a dramatic end well before the completion of its constitutional term, which had begun at the end of 1999.

---

[1] This section presents a synthesis of the conclusions of the book: M. Damill, R. Frenkel and R. Maurizio, (2002), *Argentina: Una década de convertibilidad. Un análisis del crecimiento, el empleo y la distribución del ingreso*, International Labor Office, Santiago de Chile.

The macroeconomic regime of the 1990s, including convertibility of the peso at a one-to-one rate with the U.S. dollar, is now history. An entire decade passed from the radiant initial success in April 1991 of the hard pegging of the exchange rate, to its abandonment following a protracted recession that persisted for more than three years. Presently, the Argentine economy is struggling to emerge from the many uncertainties that arose with the collapse of the prior set of economic rules and from the difficulties encountered in establishing an alternative. It faces the challenge of recovering basic macroeconomic balances in an unfavorable international context.

Argentina embraced a comprehensive economic reform effort at the beginning of the 1990s. In addition to convertibility, it included massive privatization of public utilities, deep trade and financial liberalization, equal treatment of local and foreign capital, and the deregulation of domestic markets. At first, both drastic deflation and fast economic growth seemed to prove this combination right. Other reforms, like granting autonomy to the Central Bank and reorganizing the pension system, were later implemented as additional measures to consolidate the institutional framework of the new macroeconomic setting.

From a macroeconomic perspective, two neat cycles emerge in the period from 1991 to 2001. First, the outstanding early success of price stabilization brought by a lengthy four-year expansion and the subsequent short recession in 1995. The second cycle started after 1995, with a brief recovery that was followed by the current recession in mid-1998. This recession has been characterized by an unusually long contractionary period. It has been a true depression, accompanied by a slight declining trend in nominal prices, and has led to the final crisis of the 1990s monetary regime.

Some negative signals were already discernible during the initial expansionary phase that preceded the *tequila* episode of late-1994, reflecting increased financial vulnerability due to shifts in capital inflows. In effect, well before the impact of the spillover of the Mexican crisis, some labor-market indicators began to deteriorate. In particular, the lack of dynamism in employment creation became evident as a kind of anomaly in a period of fast economic growth. Additionally, income distribution indicators, such as the incidence of unemployment among both households and individuals, were also showing an early worsening. In the second half of the 1990s, a much poorer macroeconomic performance lay behind a generalized deterioration of labor-market and income-distribution indexes. This phase led to a deep crisis and the breakdown of the system in December 2001.

Capital flows had a crucial role in the short-run macroeconomic dynamics of the period through their impact on interest rates, internal liquidity, and total expenditure. In the early 1990s, the net capital inflows exceeded the current account deficit, thus allowing for a significant accumulation of foreign reserves while feeding domestic credit creation and economic recovery. In this way, capital inflows achieved a double target: price stabilization and output growth. In contrast, significant capital outflows later triggered the recession of the mid-1990s. Renewed inflows gave impulse to the next recovery. A worsening of the international context after the crises of Southeast Asia in 1997 and Russia in 1998 stopped the economic expansion and triggered the second recession of the decade. Later, closing access to foreign credit determined the collapse of the system.

Under the convertibility framework, there was a close relationship between fluctuations in capital flows and the domestic cycle of economic activity. In this institutional context, changes in international conditions regarding liquidity and credit availability have an immediate impact on domestic interest rates, supplies of money and credit, and thus, short-run macroeconomic performance. This is a particularly disadvantageous feature, taking into account the evident volatility of international capital movements.

Effects on Employment

The above-mentioned cycles had a counterpart cycle in the labor market, and impacts on income distribution, poverty, and unemployment. Exchange rate-based stabilization processes like the Argentine one in the early-1990s – involving simultaneous trade opening, privatization, and fiscal adjustment – tend to generate dynamics also observable in other national experiences. Both employment levels and average real incomes initially grew in the early 1990s. However, in the ensuing contractionary phase, those initial effects weakened and a number of negative factors became dominant. The combination of trade opening and exchange rate appreciation and later, the reversal of aggregate expenditure's prior rise, produced persistently negative consequences.

In this manner, the ratio of full-time employment to population, after increasing from 1991 to 1992, started to fall to a new low in 1996, well below its 1990 level. By the end of the period, average real incomes of employed individuals were almost 11 percent below their 1994 level. The full-time employment ratio was about 2.7 percentage points lower in 2000 than its 1992 peak. Meanwhile, unemployment increased by 3.87 percentage points in the same period.

The contractionary adjustment of employment in the 1990s was a gradual adaptation to the trade reform and changes in relative prices instituted at the beginning of the decade. The increased competition posed by imported goods and a strong upswing in the ratio between average wages and the cost of capital goods explains a significant drop in labor demand by firms. The dominant negative effects came from the restructuring and concentration of economic activity in the tradable sectors, particularly in manufactures, as in the cases of Brazil and Mexico.

Even in expansionary periods, the increases in demand for manufactured goods could not offset the direct displacement of domestic production by imported goods nor the reduction in the number of jobs per unit of output in the surviving firms. Furthermore, many small- and medium-sized firms found they faced difficulties too arduous to continue operating; their closures were an important cause of employment contraction.

EFFECTS ON INCOME DISTRIBUTION

Estimated income distribution indicators for both households and employed individuals improved slightly in the initial period. The incidence of poverty showed an important fall from the record levels of the 1989-90 hyperinflationary phase. Unemployment, however, was different: after an initial reduction, it started to climb early on, while the economy was still in the middle of an economic expansion. This panorama seriously worsened starting in 1994. Average real incomes of both employed workers and the active population fell, significantly for the latter in particular, as a result of the simultaneous impact of lowered wages and a higher unemployment rate.

Income distribution indicators suffered a generalized and significant deterioration in the mid-1990s. The Gini index for households, for instance, recorded significant increases, as did the Gini index for employed workers and, even more intensely, that for the active population. The rising unemployment rate is the main factor explaining the deterioration in these income-distribution indexes. Unemployment affects income distribution in a number of ways. One effect is direct, diminishing the number of income recipients among active persons. Since the contraction in the number of jobs hits the lowest-income households more intensely, unemployment was not neutral to income distribution among households. Unemployment affected less educated workers more severely, these workers representing a high proportion of the lowest-income households.

The rise in unemployment also has an indirect impact on labor earnings and distribution. It causes a decline in the hourly earnings of both full-time and underemployed workers. The unemployment rate also has a negative effect on the number of hours worked by the underemployed. As the incidence of underemployment is higher in the lowest-income households, these effects had negative consequences on income distribution.

The estimated unemployment elasticities of workers' earnings are very close to those of the United States and other developed economies. This suggests that the observed increase in unemployment and underemployment cannot be attributed to a particularly strong downward inflexibility of wages. From 1998, for instance, average earnings fell somewhat, amid a slight negative trend in nominal prices, without any significant positive effect on employment levels. On the contrary, it is possible that these factors generated greater excess supply in the goods markets, thus reinforcing the depression in the labor market. On the one hand, lower earnings have a negative impact on aggregate demand. On the other hand, price deflation increases the level of debts in real terms. This can also have a negative effect on aggregate expenditures, through its impact on debtors' spending propensities (investment projects, fall in future expected cash-flows, etc.).

An intermittent pro-cyclical fiscal policy added to these depressive factors in recent years, particularly starting in late 1999, when public-sector access to foreign credit became increasingly difficult. Economic malaise has also been manifested in the lack of policy instruments to help the economy emerge from its setting of depression and price deflation.

After deterioration in the mid-1990s, the estimated income distribution indicators recorded a moderate improvement in the ensuing expansion between 1996 and 1998. During this phase, average incomes of both employed workers and active individuals rose, but they never reached 1994 pre-*tequila* crisis levels. After 1998, and the spillover of the Russian crisis, macroeconomic performance clearly worsened.

At the beginning of the 1990s, exchange rate appreciation, combined with trade opening, crucially affected the behavior of labor indicators. In the second half of the decade, other factors such as sustained deficits in the current account of the balance of payments and the accumulation of foreign debt played a dominant role.

The burden of the debt was another constraint to growth that reinforced the negative effect of firms' low profitability in the tradable sectors. The combination of higher financial fragility with an unfavorable shift in the international scene led to a significant decline in private capital inflows, starting in 1998. The accumulation of foreign reserves stopped, negatively impacting on domestic liquidity and pushing up interest rates. A new economic contraction followed, as well as a decline in the average real earnings of both the employed workers and the active population.

Unemployment and poverty indicators also resumed their rise in 1998-2000. Poverty has nearly returned to 1991 levels and unemployment has risen between the beginning and end of the decade. Looking ahead, the consequences of the crisis will certainly include an additional worsening of labor conditions and income distribution.

In summary, comparing 1991 and 2001:

• Full-time urban employment fell by 1.8 percentage points, largely in the manufacturing sector, and the proportion of male and head-of-household workers in manufacturing decreased.

• The proportion of involuntarily underemployed persons rose by more than 3 percentage points. As a consequence, the employment rate, including the underemployed, increased by slightly more than 1 point.

• The only sector to generate a relatively important number of full-time jobs was financial services.

• The proportion of active individuals in the total population followed a sustained upward trend. This ratio increased by about 1 percentage point every three years in the 1990s, with increasing female labor participation.

• Weak employment creation, together with rising numbers of active individuals, explains the large upward shift in the unemployment rate. It rose from 6.3% of the active population at the beginning of 1991 to 14.7% by late 2000.

• Per capita real income of the employed was almost 9% higher by the end of the period, but was almost unchanged for the active population, reflecting the upward shift in participation rates.

• Although the average earnings of employed workers rose (by less than 10%), several indicators show that their distribution worsened considerably. This is due in part to the distributive effects of the rise in the unemployment rate.

• The number of full-time jobs declined.

• The participation of female workers and people with higher education also rose. Workers with secondary-level education also increased as a share of the total, but in a lower proportion, while those with only primary-level education lost ground. These trends in employment figures closely followed the changes in the educational levels of the total population. A major increase in the returns of education is also observable in the period.

• Distribution indicators like the Gini index for households, as well as those for poverty and unemployment, showed markedly rising trends in all cases. The income of the richest decile of households was 40.3% of total income in 2000, while it had been only 35.3% in 1991. This income was equivalent to 23.6 times the total earnings of the lowest-income decile of households in 1991, but in 2000, it was 38% times that of the lowest-income decile.

These dramatic shifts in labor indicators and income distribution were not the result of the final crisis of the macroeconomic regime of the 1990s in Argentina, but had preceded the crisis.

SOME HYPOTHESES ON THE CRISIS

The above assessment attributes the reasons for the process almost exclusively to macroeconomic factors. If political errors are ranked according to their relative

41

importance, the Menem and De la Rúa Administrations hold primary responsibility for setting up and supporting the convertibility regime. The same should be said about the IMF, which supported the sacred dogma with financial resources, gave its seal of approval to unsustainable programs, and provided arguments in defense of the currency board.

Before abandoning the boat just as it was sinking, the IMF encouraged policy measures that contributed to deepening the recession and pushing the economy further into a vicious circle of sales and activity contractions reducing tax collection and causing a further deterioration in fiscal accounts. Both the authorities and the IMF followed this line, disregarding sensible analyses, international experience, and the overwhelming evidence of a persistent worsening of the country's economic and social situation.

From 1991, the Argentine macroeconomic framework consisted of trade and financial liberalization, a currency board regime ruling the exchange rate and monetary policies, a partial but increasing dollarization of the banking system, and a strongly appreciated exchange rate. The results of Argentine performance are essentially the same that were observed in Argentina and Chile in the late seventies and early eighties and more recently in Mexico between 1988 and 1994, and in Brazil between 1994 and 1998.

In all these cases, a cycle developed: an expansionary phase followed by a period of stagnation or recession, increasing external and financial fragility, and finally, a financial and exchange rate crisis. A decline in the number of workers in the tradable and formal sectors, rise in unemployment and/or employment in the informal sector, and deterioration in income distribution were also common features.

Argentina experienced the cycle twice in the decade, because the convertibility regime survived the 1995 *tequila* crisis. After 1995, the economy underwent another short expansionary phase backed by a new surge in capital flows that lasted until the 1997 Asian crisis. Because of the first cycle, high external debt ratios and a high unemployment rate composed the initial conditions of the second cycle.

An appreciated exchange rate and partial dollarization of the local banking system are not necessary ingredients of a currency board regime. They arose from specific local circumstances, but both constituted basic characteristics of the convertibility regime and significantly influenced its performance.

The appreciated exchange rate was a crucial factor. The exchange rate was greatly appreciated when it was pegged to the dollar in 1991. From a highly depreciated exchange rate in early 1990 amidst hyperinflation, the exchange rate appreciated significantly that year. There was a slight depreciation in the late 1990s, but the changes did not significantly alter the appreciated level, which persisted through the period. There was a significant increase in manufacturing sector labor productivity, but the average unit labor cost in constant dollars did not fall because the prices of non-tradable goods and services and nominal wages rose in the first half of the 1990s. Fluctuations in the multilateral real exchange rate were mainly the result of exchange rate fluctuations of trade partners, particularly Brazil.

The partial dollarization of the domestic financial system is an important factor, and explains both the persistence of the system and the complexity of the present financial crisis. The Convertibility Law sanctioned the validity of monetary contracts denominated in any currency. The measure was originally intended to encourage the repatriation of

Argentine capital, allowing their owners to make deposits in dollars in domestic banks. Despite the high credibility enjoyed by the exchange rate commitment, as measured by the interest rate differentials, private sector savers preferred dollar-denominated deposits while banks hedged – or so they thought – balance sheets against exchange rate risk by offering dollar-denominated credits. Consequently, from the start of the convertibility regime, there was a persistently growing proportion of dollar-denominated assets and liabilities in the local banking system.

The dollarization of local savings and credits played important roles in agents' perceptions and behavior. Both the public and the banks perceived the dollarization of private sector assets as a hedge against the risk of devaluation (wrongly, because both disregarded the existence of a systemic exchange risk) and so contributed to stabilizing local portfolios. On the other hand, the exchange risk burden rested not only on foreign investors, banks, and large firms indebted abroad, but also on numerous local bank debtors with peso-denominated income. Later, this feature greatly amplified the wealth effects and forced authorities to implement a massive intervention in private financial contracts.

While the Argentine experience resembles other cases of trade and financial liberalization with exchange rate appreciation, the negative consequences of financial globalization in Argentina were more accentuated than in other countries. The convertibility regime was extremely rigid, not just as legal rules but also in the actual market behavior. For instance, the flexibility of the real exchange rate vis-à-vis negative external shocks would have required a significant downward flexibility of domestic non-tradable goods prices. Actually, no significant nominal deflation took place either in the 1995 recession or in 1998-2001, despite the significant flexibility of wages.

The convertibility regime determined two features of macroeconomic performance. First, there was a growing external gap: the combination of the opening up of trade and an appreciated exchange rate has produced a chronic trade balance deficit. The trade balance reached equilibrium or surplus only under conditions of deep recession. On the other hand, there was a growing structural deficit in the services account, caused by debt accumulation and foreign capital investment. Consequently, the system increased the current account deficit. This means that the economy required substantial net capital inflows to reach a positive rate of growth; indeed, the economy required increasing external capital inflows to sustain *any* positive rate of growth.

Second, the volatility of the international financial conditions that the country confronted was mechanically transmitted to domestic activity and employment. The correlation between national performance and the behavior of international capital markets is a common characteristic of emerging market economies, as was dramatically illustrated in the second half of the 1990s. In the Argentine case, the convertibility regime accentuated the correlation because it lacked monetary and nominal flexibility. In the first half of the 1990s, capital inflows and consumption led a boom in domestic demand. The Argentine economy was the hardest hit in Latin America by Mexico's devaluation and the *tequila* crisis, with the second deepest regional recession after Mexico's. A second surge in capital inflows led to accelerated growth in 1996-97. The external impulse slowed after October 1997, together with the rate of growth. There was again a turnaround in economic activity in the third quarter of 1998, after the Russian-Brazilian crisis − but well before the Brazilian devaluation in January 1999. In 1999, Argentina confronted international financial conditions similar to those of Brazil, as

indicated by the country-risk premium. The Argentine economy suffered one of the deepest recessions in the region –
only Ecuador and Venezuela ranked below Argentina.

To some extent, the currency board regime overstated
its intended role as an automatic stabilizer of external
accounts. The balance of payments deficit caused an
automatic contraction in money and credit, a fall in aggregate demand and a consequent contraction in imports. In
the convertibility regime, however, the deepest recessions
left the current account with a substantial deficit and a very
high unemployment rate. These features weigh negatively
on international investors' perceptions and tend to compensate for its positive aspects. The Argentine version of
the currency board far from moderated the risk of default.

The investor community had to express opinions and
bet on the risk of default and the permanence of the convertibility regime. Default and/or the abandonment of the
convertibility regime were among the potential outcomes
of the Argentine case. This characteristic put the economy
in a multiple-equilibrium situation, vulnerable to self-fulfilling prophecies. Multiple-equilibrium situations and self-
fulfilling prophecies are not unusual in the present setting
of international financial markets. One difference between
Argentina and other emerging markets was the reduced
relevance of domestic economic factors in Argentina.
Given the features of the macroeconomic performance
mentioned thus far, what counted most for sustainability
were external factors.

These external factors included, for instance, those
that most affected the prospects for the balance of trade:
export commodity prices and Brazilian demand for
Argentine imports. Fundamentals contributed only partially, however, to the formation of the players' assessment of
market conditions. Given that the bulk of the financial
needs involved financing debt rollover and the deficit in

the factor services account, the most important assessment for individual players focused on the future behavior of the international financial market with respect to Argentina. The signals about the prospects for the balance of trade – like any other signals – were valued mainly for their expected influence on the financial market's future behavior.

Because the convertibility regime gave little room for correcting policies, the government's "economic policy" was restricted to delivering signals. The importance of government economic measures lay mainly in their presumed signaling value. Fiscal adjustment and fiscal equilibrium commitments, for instance, were credibility signals of sure value, despite their negative impact on aggregate demand. For instance, an agreement with the IMF weighed more as a market signal than for the amount of resources committed.

It has already been mentioned that an acute dependency on external capital inflows was the original sin of the convertibility regime. Sustainability and growth expectations fluctuated throughout the 1990s, driven by good and bad news. The Mexican crisis contagion disappointed the initial expectations of persistently high capital inflows and revealed their volatility. At the same time, booming commodity prices and the Brazilian *real* plan represented good news. Helped by the positive real shock and an $11 billion rescue package, the convertibility regime survived the *tequila* effect. The combination of both a favorable real external environment and the very success of the rescue operation gave strength to unfounded optimistic expectations and a new surge in private capital inflows that lasted until the Asian crisis. From then on, optimism receded, capital inflows declined, and the country risk premium rose persistently, with relative high peaks marked by the Russian-Brazilian crises and the Brazilian devaluation.

In 1998-99, as the financial conditions of the emerging markets reflected the aftermath of the Asian crisis, the main real external factors of the Argentine economy, including the bilateral *real* exchange rate vis-à-vis Brazil, all turned for the worse. Without any compensating effects of external good news, analysts once again saw in Argentina the uncompetitiveness of its economy. The October 2000 agreement with the IMF spurred the last wave of moderate optimism – this tempered optimism lasting only a month.

On no occasion throughout this turbulent history was an eventual withdrawal from the convertibility regime put under serious public discussion. Although criticism arose from time to time, no significant political or social representative publicly called for a change of system. Similarly, few economists criticized or even focused their analysis of Argentina's problems on the difficulties embodied in the system. In the public arena, the convertibility regime was taken as a given and inalterable state of nature. It became a sacred dogma not to be discussed in rational terms. Critics carried the burden of being labeled as "devaluationist" and were doomed to intellectual and political isolation.

On the other hand, some influential economists strongly supported the system. Their arguments did not disregard the negative evidence but emphasized the virtues of discipline it imposed on the Argentine government and society. With time, these virtues were expected to bear fruits in competitiveness, higher exports, and sustainable growth. Sectoral interests help to explain the situation. Banks, large firms indebted abroad, foreign-owned companies, and financial intermediaries were strongly interested in continuity. Domestic credit dollarization vastly expanded this interest. Analyses and opinions were not immune to those influences.

Leaving aside faith and interests, it is fair to say that a change in the convertibility regime would, in any case, have been a very difficult and risky policy move. Acceleration of inflation was a real threat. The fear of inflation constituted the main source of popular adherence to the fixed exchange rate to such a point that convertibility and price stability were almost interchangeable terms in the public arena. Change in the local financial system seemed no less difficult and risky.

In addition to technical complexities, a change of regime would have entailed political risks as well. Those in office at the time would have surely carried the full burden of responsibility and been blamed by popular opinion for short-run disruptions and negative consequences. Thus, it could be said that most of public attitudes, opinions, and silence were driven more by fear than by conviction. Finally, as in most similar situations, the crisis, not a decision, put an end to the convertibility regime.

3

THE ARGENTINE CRISIS: A BANKING CRISIS OR MACRO-ECONOMIC CRISIS?

NICOLÁS DUJOVNE

In this chapter, I will discuss the background to the crisis and the issues that must be addressed to improve the situation in Argentina. The events of the current crisis have their roots in the history of the 1990s; I will present my thoughts on how these years have affected present-day Argentina.

Argentina's economy did very well during 1991-98, with an average annual GDP growth rate of 5.5%. This was a clear improvement compared to the 1980s, when GDP fell at a half percent a year. After the second quarter of 1998, however, GDP began to contract at a rate of 4.8%, a decline that is now accelerating. Growth in the 1990s is closely connected to macro-economic reforms, with trade and capital account liberalization, privatization, improvement in the provincial framework within the financial system, and reform of the pension system. There were also some fiscal improvements since the 1980s, reflected in the financial spreads that Argentina had to pay on its external borrowings. Of course, it was also reflected in the rising capital inflows of the private sector, which are perfectly correlated with the evolution of the GDP.

This history is complicated by both indigenous and exogenous factors. Argentina did very well in some aspects, but also benefited from the boom of the emerging markets and the money it brought to Latin America. During that period, Argentina posted a negative result in its fiscal accounts, especially after 1994, and primary surpluses never exceeded 1% of GDP.

From 1991 to 1995, primary expenditures by both the federal government and the provinces rose markedly, accompanied by a large increase in tax collection as the economy grew rapidly. The overall figures for the deficit are not very different from those in Mexico and other Latin American success stories. However, after the external shocks of 1997, with the Asian crisis, devaluations, the Russian default, and the Brazilian *real* devaluation, those fiscal outcomes were not enough.

The observed primary surpluses that Argentina posted and the required primary surpluses that Argentina needed to stabilize the debt-to-GDP ratio were in balance until 1998. In 1999, the country required an adjustment of half a percentage of GDP to stabilize the ratio. In 2000, GDP adjustment became two points of GDP on the primary surplus, and finally, in 2001, an impossible four-point adjustment was required on the fiscal and primary surplus.

This was the result of debt accumulation over the decade under rising average interest rates on the debt, maturity of debt incurred in the 1980s, debt rollover at current market rates, and the very slow growth of the economy. Using the average of the last three years to forecast the future growth of the economy, it became apparent that the necessary primary surpluses were much higher than observed. The authorities showed very little interest in making even small fiscal adjustments when necessary.

Ultimately, the size of the adjustment was too high, which explains why Argentina's debt-to-GDP ratio started to diverge from those observed in comparable economies such as Mexico and Brazil. Argentina had performed better than Brazil in terms of the debt-to-GDP ratio until 1999 but then found itself on an unsustainable path while the other countries were solving their fiscal problems.

This diagnosis takes us to the beginning of the year 2000. However, the authorities who took office at the beginning of 2001 did not share this diagnosis. Perhaps they believed that the necessary fiscal adjustment was possible or perhaps they had a different diagnosis. In any case, they pursued a different policy that included the following regarding monetary and fiscal institutions:
• violation of Central Bank independence,
• use of international reserves to finance the Treasury,
• change in framework of and interference in pension funds,
• a reduction in bank capital and liquidity through debt swaps,
• discounts to public banks to finance government deficits,
• creation of quasi-currencies in the provinces,
• introduction of expanded convertibility,
• interest rate controls,
• freeze on deposits, and
• restrictions on the use of cash, and exchange controls.

Regarding fiscal institutions, the following measures were taken:
• the decision to not present the budget to Congress,
• the violation of the fiscal responsibility laws,
• the violation of laws regulating the relation between federal provinces and the government,

- frequent changes in taxes,
- frequent tax moratoria,
- discretionary competitiveness plans,
- lack of fiscal transparency,
- inconsistency of plans announced with the IMF, and
- an increasing deficit.

In addition, the government adopted high levels of protectionism through the increase in tariffs and trade barriers, the delegation of special powers to the presidency, weakening the role of Congress, and rhetoric against foreign investors and financial systems. All of this took place in a context of weak political and presidential authority.

It is therefore not surprising to see plummeting consumer confidence, industrial production, and credit. This occurred very quickly, and was accompanied by the public sector capturing the largest share of credit at the expense of the private sector. Deposits thus fell, because there was a huge run of money out of Argentina.

Finally, of course, tax revenue collapsed. What had started as a small fiscal problem two years earlier ended as a debacle for government accounts. So what can we expect this year? If we are very optimistic, GDP will fall by a minimum of 10%. The pass-through from the effects, from exchange rates to prices, may be more or less one-third. My numbers show that the current account balance will show more or less a $10 billion surplus, which means an 8% surplus in terms of GDP. This shows a tremendous shift in capital flows, going from a two-point deficit in 2001 to an eight-point surplus in 2002. So it is a shift of more than 10% of GDP. In a very closed economy such as Argentina's, this is consistent with a huge fall in GDP to make imports go down.

What issues have to be addressed to build for the future? One is the financial system in terms of capital and liquidity. The other is the restructuring of debt. Starting with the latter, the government must announce what Argentina will do with its debt and then try to fulfill its targets. It must have a credible fiscal program and then an accompanying, consistent monetary program. Then, the government must decide on sector reforms, legal reforms, and the kind of IMF program that would fit within the strategy of the government.

I want to go a bit deeper into the financial system and the strategy of the government. When the Duhalde government took office, the damage was already done; it is not guilty of the current situation. The strategy of the government was to try to keep the exchange rate under control, with moderate inflation. But I think there are some inconsistencies between the government's strategy and what is transpiring in Argentina now. The government announced a program of printing money for this year. Yet every month, 3 billion pesos are leaving the financial system while the fiscal accounts continue to be in deficit. The deficit will run to at least 5 to 7 billion pesos for this year, even taking new taxes on exports into account.

Therefore, it seems the monetary program is not consistent with reality and that the government will have to print some more money this year. That means high inflation, a low exchange rate for the peso, and a more devalued currency. As with the law of gravity, we will have inflation because with Argentina in default, the only means of financing will be printing money.

The exchange rate level that would take the Argentine economy to a zero deficit is around 4 or 4.5 pesos per dollar, with primary spending falling from about 19 to 13% of GDP. If the government recognizes the problem and announces a credible monetary program printing much beyond 3.5 billion pesos this year, it would solve the fiscal problem. There would be a system with liquidity for the banks, to dismiss the restrictions on transactions and on access to deposits by the end of the year. Thus, Argentina will have solved some problems and will then have to deal with inflation, but that can be done with measures such as an inflation-targeting program.

Another issue to be addressed by the government that is costly in terms of inflation is the situation of the privatized utilities corporations, which have debt denominated in dollars and prices specified without any adjustments. One option for the government is to accept a massive Chapter 11 bankruptcy of these companies, but that is not a good solution. Perhaps the government will have to accept some increases in the rates of the public utilities in pesos, even when they abandon the dollarized contracts and even if it is inflationary. That would circumvent another big problem for the government: holding all the public utilities in its hands.

In terms of the banks' balance sheets, there is a problem of currency mismatch after *pesification*, the transformation by law of dollar-denominated savings into pesos, which also requires attention. The banks had a net position in dollars that was relatively high prior to devaluation. The asymmetrical modification of contracts finished with that net position that was positive in dollars, exposing the financial system to decreases in equity as the exchange rate depreciates.

Finally, the present financial structure of Argentina is not viable. After the current crisis, people will not deposit money in the banks. A proposal is needed to regain confidence and avoid future problems. One possibility is the creation of a bank holding company with two subsidiaries. One subsidiary could be a commercial bank that would have only transactional deposits and very short-term deposits on the liability side, and on the assets side, mainly external assets of the best-quality Argentine corporate bonds and very short-term government public bonds. The other subsidiary would be an investment bank very similar to the banks existing before the crisis. It would capture term deposits and provide credit to the private sector.

The advantage of this structure is that a crisis would not interrupt the chain of payments and overdrafts for small- and medium-sized enterprises again. The assets of the commercial bank would be liquid and of very high quality, and the resolution process, in case illiquidity appears in the investment bank subsidiary, would be easy to solve because the two banks would be instantly isolated. The two banks would work together, but personnel should be assigned to one or the other bank at the establishment of the institution. If a resolution process is later required it would be very easy to separate both entities. Argentina would not lose transactional deposits or the chain of payments, which in the end, was the main driver of the extraordinary economic contraction that the country currently faces.

Two final points deserve mention: first, Argentina did not suffer a banking crisis – rather, Argentina suffered a macro crisis. The last step in that crisis became the banking crisis because it was previously very liquid, very solvent, maybe a bit expensive, but a very strong banking system. It was the liquid reserves in the banking system that account for the fact that Argentina's economy was still functioning for all of 2001.

4

THE ARGENTINE CRISIS
VIEWED FROM MERCOSUR

JOSÉ MARCIO CAMARGO

Understanding the Argentine crisis leads clearly to the question of the currency board. Why did the country decide to maintain this policy, even after it was clear that the fiscal adjustment implied by the currency board to make it sustainable, was politically and socially unacceptable for society?

One answer to this question is that since the beginning of the eighties, after the Martínez de Hoz experience with an overvalued currency, Argentina never had a full currency. A large percentage of the population in the country never regained confidence in a national currency. As a result, the population never really used the peso as a store of value and a large share of financial savings was made in dollars. The peso was a unit of account and, together with the dollar, a medium of exchange, but never a store of value, signaling the low degree of its credibility. This phenomenon seemed to persist even into the late 1990s and early 2000s, after a decade of monetary stability.

Without confidence in the currency, the only reason the population was willing to use the peso as a store of value during the 1990s was the currency board. Without the currency board, all financial assets would be denominated in dollars. It was commonly believed that if the government decided to leave the currency board, there would be a flight from pesos to dollars, a rapid devaluation of the peso, and the possibility that this could generate hyperinflation in the country.

The tragedy of the Argentine situation was that as the peso was not a full currency, a large share of assets was denominated in dollars. This made it impossible for the market to devalue the currency, as happened with the Mexican peso in 1994 and the Brazilian real in 1999. As total peso-denominated assets were smaller than reserves, an attack against the currency would have a low probability of success, except if the Central Bank decided not to sustain the value of the peso, which was illegal. This meant that the market would not be willing to try such an attack. Thus, the decision to devalue and leave the currency board had to be a political decision, taken by the government. The only other way out of the currency board would have been if economic conditions deteriorated to the point that the public's weakened confidence in financial institutions produced a run against the banking system. In such a case, without a lender of last resort, either the banking system would default or the currency board would have to go.

Given the high short-run costs of devaluation in a country with little faith in its own currency, this decision was postponed. When economic conditions deteriorated, the population started to view the currency board as unsustainable, generating a run against the banks and the introduction of the *corralito*, a policy restricting bank withdrawals to limit large capital outflows, in December 2001 as a defensive measure. In other words, lack of a political will to leave the currency board generated the current financial crisis. The *corralito* and *pesification* destroyed what credibility was left in the national currency and Argentina's financial system. Without credibility, there is no currency and no financial system – without these two institutions, a deep and prolonged recession is inevitable.

Why did the currency board become unsustainable after ten years? There were both internal and external reasons. On the external front, the devaluation of the Brazilian *real* was certainly a very important factor. The second important external factor was the depreciation of the euro. Since Brazil and Europe were the main trading partners of Argentina, these currency movements reduced the competitiveness of the Argentine economy.

However, the most important factor determining the fate of the currency board was the incompatibility between the currency board and the country's fiscal system. With a currency board, it is impossible to maintain a fiscal deficit for long, since generating inflation by printing money is not an option. Critically, as economic conditions deteriorated, the fiscal system also deteriorated. Since the Central Bank could not print money, the provinces started to do so to cover their expenses. As a result, at the end of the process, the country had neither a credible fiscal budget nor a monetary authority.

The fiscal dimension of the crisis is particularly relevant. The problem is not only the ability to execute a sustainable fiscal policy in the short run, but to have a structure of revenues and expenditures – between the different levels of government, provinces, municipalities, and the federal government – that can generate fiscal responsibility in the long run. Argentina lacked such a structure throughout the past decade. Argentina lacks something even more basic than fiscal equilibrium – a sustainable and credible fiscal system.

The collapse of the currency board, combined with all the policies adopted so far, have generated two other problems: first the collapse of the Argentine political and judicial system and second, the insolvency of the banking sector. Thus, Argentina must now reconstruct at least *five fundamental institutions* for the functioning of the economy and a democratic society: a political system, a judicial system, a credible currency, a structured and sustainable fiscal system, and a financial system.

Is this reconstruction possible without further political and economic disruption? Where should the process begin – from the fiscal system? How can this be done if the federal government does not have enough political support to impose a new fiscal structure on the provinces? From an international perspective, how can the international financial organizations lend money to a country whose federal government is unable to control its budget? How can a credible currency be constructed if a sustainable fiscal system is not in place? These questions require urgent answers if Argentina is to avoid further political and economic disruption.

THE CRISIS AND MERCOSUR

But why is it so important for the other countries in MERCOSUR that Argentina recover from this crisis as fast as possible? The reason is simple. Brazil and Argentina are relatively closed and, at the same time, relatively indebted economies. They have relatively high ratios of current account deficits to trade volume (export plus import), making their economies vulnerable to changes at the whim of investors and thus, the direction of capital. Current account deficits must be financed either through capital inflows or through a trade surplus. If this ratio is high, the relative change in the trade surplus needed to compensate for the change in capital flows is also high. With capital much more volatile than trade, the result is that the countries become overly vulnerable to changes in capital flows, as the necessary adjustment in their real sector (output and imports) to compensate for a reduction in capital inflows is very high. The costs of these adjustments are also very high, with reductions in output and increases in unemployment. This set of factors makes the country too risky for international investors.

The reduction of this ratio can be achieved by reducing the current account deficit or by increasing the volume of trade or both. But Argentina's current account deficit is in foreign savings and, with difficulties in increasing domestic savings in the short-run paired with the goal of increasing investment and growth, it is difficult to imagine how these objectives could be reached without generating inflation if savings decline. The solution then, is an increase in the volume of trade.

This is where the Free Trade Area of the Americas (FTAA) becomes important. The negotiations for the FTAA are scheduled to start by the end of 2002. This will be a difficult negotiation, given the opposition of the U.S. Congress to open its agricultural and agribusiness sector and reduce subsidies to these sectors. On the other hand, Brazil and Argentina have important interests in these sectors. Both countries are very competitive in many of the segments that are heavily subsidized and protected by the U.S. government. Besides agriculture and agribusiness, other important sectors for both countries are industrial commodities and natural resource-based sectors. Sectors like mining, iron, steel, cellulose, paper, etc. are very important for both countries and many are protected areas of U.S. trade.

Brazil and Argentina together are very small compared to the U.S. economy. A relatively small liberalization in trade would mean a sharp increase in trade between the two countries and the United States. A sharp increase in trade could be the easiest way to reduce the external vulnerability of both countries and increase growth. Furthermore, the negotiating positions of both countries toward this end would be much bolstered if Argentina's economy and society were to be much more robust than they currently are.

Thus, it is very important for the future of the MERCOSUR countries that Argentina be able to emerge from the crisis as soon as possible. This does not mean a return to a growth trajectory, but resolution of the five fundamental institutional problems described above. These institutions lay the precondition for growth and for Argentina to become a strong partner within MERCOSUR in the FTAA negotiation process.

5

THE ARGENTINE CRISIS IN INTERNATIONAL PERSPECTIVE

ANDRÉS SOLIMANO

COMPARING CRISES

The Argentine crisis of late 2001 and early 2002, following the collapse of the currency board, has been marked by a severe disorganization of the economy, in which:

• the national currency has depreciated by more than 70% in three months,

• inflation and unemployment are rising,

• the banking system is unable to meet its obligations with depositors and foreign creditors,

• real gross domestic product is expected to contract about 15% during 2002,

• there are major demonstrations of popular discontent involving not only the unemployed and popular classes but also the middle class, which is infuriated by the failure of the banks to honor their deposits, and

• Argentina has had three Presidents since December of

2001 when the crisis erupted and the democratically elected President Fernando de la Rúa resigned.

In sum, Argentina is experiencing a national crisis encompassing the economy, the social fabric of the country, and the political system.

From an international perspective, this crisis fits within a series of crises that began in the 1990s. In the developing world,[1] there have been several crises in the 1990s and early 2000s: Mexico in late 1994 and 1995, Asia in 1997-98, Russia in 1998, Brazil in 1999, Turkey in 2000, and now Argentina. Currency and financial crises are frequent and intense and seem to extend, in many cases, to other countries. In turn, the recoveries seem to be faster than initially expected; this was at least the case in Mexico, Korea and other Asian countries, Russia, and Brazil.

The current Argentine crisis shares some common elements with these other crises: it started with the collapse of a fixed exchange rate regime with the currency depreciating sharply, followed by an often severe fall in output and a rise in unemployment. The severity of Argentina's economic contraction seems high compared to other crises of the last decade. The Argentine case also involves a banking crisis, in which an important segment of the banking system has both negative net worth and acute liquidity problems to pay depositors. The economic crisis also has a political dimension, in which the sequence of presidential resignations, the level of massive popular discontent, and the distrust of political elites is of remarkable virulence. A parallel can be made with the political aftermath in Indonesia in the mid- to late 1990s.

---

[1] The industrialized economies have also experienced a currency crisis, with the crisis of the British pound and the European Exchange Rate Mechanism in 1992.

An important difference between the current Argentine crisis and the other crises of the last decade is the degree of the external response by international financial institutions, such as the International Monetary Fund. After the onset of the Mexican and Asian crises, the IMF almost immediately put in place large packages of financial assistance to rescue these economies. Substantial bilateral financial help complemented these packages – from the U.S., in the case of Mexico. In Argentina, the 2000-01 "rescue package" came *before* the full crisis erupted. The IMF money was intended to sustain the convertibility board. However, once the currency regime collapsed and Argentina entered a full crisis, IMF aid has not been forthcoming.

A comparison between crises in Argentina and Chile is useful. In the early 1980s, Chile also suffered an economic crisis of similar proportions to Argentina's current crisis. The Chilean crisis of 1982-83[2] had the following features:

• several currency devaluations,

• a severe banking crisis (the consolidated banking system lost between one-third and 40 percent of its net worth),

• GDP declined by a cumulative 15 percent in the years 1982-83, and

• open unemployment climbed to around 23 percent of the labor force in 1983 (close to 30 percent if emergency employment programs are included).

However, the fiscal position of Chile in 1982 was better than that of Argentina in 2002. At the political level, the Chilean crisis and its sequence of high unemployment, a banking crisis, and deteriorated living standards triggered

---

[2] See Solimano (1991)

the first serious, massive social challenge to the military regime of General Augusto Pinochet, setting into motion a democratizing process. Some of Chile's banking system recovery policies and its emergency employment programs might be useful to Argentina in its current situation.

LESSONS FROM
THE ARGENTINE CRISIS

Several lessons for stabilization and reform can be drawn from the crisis in Argentina:
• Currency boards can work well, initially, to stop inflation but can later become a straitjacket to adjustment.
• Public finances and debt levels need to be sustainable.
• Social protection mechanisms need to accompany economic reform.
• The stability and solvency of the financial system is crucial.
• Political and institutional reform must parallel economic reform.

The *currency board* put in place in Argentina in 1991 was very important to stop inflation, restore stability, lower interest rates, and enable growth recovery for a few years. The currency board later proved, however, too rigid to respond to adverse external developments, such as the sharp depreciation of the Brazilian *real* in 1999, the appreciation of the dollar, and a cut-off of external finance to Latin America in the late 1990s.

The general lesson here is not that currency boards are always doomed to fail. Currency boards have been successfully adopted in Estonia and Bulgaria in the 1990s, and previously in Hong Kong and in some other nations. However, the Argentine case shows that currency boards may pose very serious problems for a smooth adjustment of the economy to adverse shocks because they rely on deflationary internal adjustment of wages and prices that can be too costly to implement[3].

The *fiscal deficit and accumulation of internal and external debt* are considered the main contributors to most of Argentina's current problems. The theory of balance of payments crisis[4] hypothesizes that fiscal imbalances are inconsistent with a fixed exchange rate regime. Although Argentina ran primary fiscal surpluses in recent years, its overall fiscal position was in deficit because of the interest payments component of the internal and external debt held by the government. In addition, the reform of social security undertaken in the 1990s imposed a significant fiscal burden and the complex system of revenue sharing with the provinces tended to strain public finances. Argentina's case confirms Krugman's analysis of the currency crisis, that a fiscal deficit is ultimately inconsistent with a fixed exchange rate regime. In addition, the recourse in recent years to internal and external borrowing to defend a fixed exchange rate parity at high interest rates was a risky policy that worsened the fiscal balance. It left a serious burden to future generations and weakened the banking system.

Argentina's current crisis also exposes the utterly *precarious nature of its institutions of social protection.* Unemployment insurance coverage is low and the system

---

[3] See Eichengreen, B. (1996) and Beckerman and Solimano (2002, forthcoming).

[4] See Krugman (1979).

is unable to cope with massive unemployment. Income transfer mechanisms do not work because of a lack of resources. Furthermore, the banking crisis prevented depositors from using their savings to maintain consumption in the wake of falling real incomes. For these reasons, currently, both social insurance and private insurance (i.e., individual savings) are severely curtailed.

A lesson here is that in good times – and Argentina enjoyed good times at various points in the 1990s – the government must build networks and institutions of social protection to help people cope when bad times occur. Argentina has now found itself without adequate social protection mechanisms at a time when they are badly needed. These mechanisms could have been built during more prosperous times when more fiscal resources were available.

The *Argentine banking system* was already strained before the collapse of the currency board. The combination of recession and high interest rates had deteriorated the position of debtors (i.e., households and firms), raising the proportion of non-recoverable loans and worsening the balance sheets of banks, which were forced to invest in government paper. When the currency board was finally abandoned and the peso sharply depreciated, banks were caught with part of their assets (i.e., loans) in pesos and their liabilities (chiefly, deposits) in dollars. The severity of the recession and the run on deposits have further aggravated the already deteriorated situation of the banks.

Finally, *the role of politics* needs to be understood. Lack of transparency, a number of financial scandals involving former government officials, and a low level of trust by the public in parliament and political parties, all reflect the absence of social cohesion and institutional credibility in Argentina today. As with social protection, the lack of confidence in political institutions makes the process of economic reform more difficult and endangers the country's sense of democracy.

POLICIES FOR RESTORING STABILITY, GROWTH AND SOCIAL PEACE IN ARGENTINA

Argentina needs a coherent economic plan to restore stability, recover growth, and preserve social peace. As many historical examples show, both in Latin America and elsewhere, protracted economic crises can threaten democracy and open the door to authoritarian regimes. That was the case of Central Europe in the 1920s[5], particularly Germany, where hyperinflation and economic disorganization led to the disintegration of the Weimar Republic and opened the door to Nazism. In Latin America in the 1970s, the onset of military regimes, as in Argentina in 1976, very often coincided with serious economic crises. In fact, the inability of civilian governments to cope with ongoing economic crises was, in those days, one of the army's standard justifications for taking power.

A coherent economic plan for Argentina must focus on:
• stabilizing the exchange rate and domestic inflation,
• restoring the solvency of the banking system and ensuring a normal payments system,
• ensuring fiscal sustainability,

---

[5] See Solimano (1990, 1991) for historical analyses of stabilization.

- enabling a recovery of growth and a decline in unemployment, and
- normalizing relations with external creditors.

These objectives must be supplemented with an emergency social policy oriented to supporting income levels, ensuring food security, and providing jobs to those suffering the effects of the economic crisis: the unemployed, the vulnerable (the elderly, children, etc.), and low-income families. Assuaging the middle class, which is enraged by the loss of savings, also becomes a social and financial policy priority if social conflict is to be avoided.

A program with the IMF can help to meet some of these objectives, but the country needs to carefully negotiate the policy conditionality of such a program in order to avoid introducing additional strains on an already extremely volatile social situation. The amount of net external resources in an eventual IMF program also needs assessment. A variety of policy instruments and programs can be, in principle, consistent with the economic and social objectives stated above. International experience with successful stabilizations in both Latin America and elsewhere can be a reference point for designing and implementing adequate economic policies with due attention to the specifics and institutions of the Argentine reality. Finally, it is important to mention that both the international community and Argentines need to act together to pull the country out of its current crisis. External resources are badly needed, as well as credible assurances that reasonable internal policies will be in place and foreign money will be properly used. Domestic consensus around a program of national recovery is essential. At the same time, the international community cannot be a passive bystander to the crisis, whose consequences for regional and global prosperity and democracy go well beyond Argentina. It is time for all relevant actors to act now.

REFERENCES

Beckerman, P. and Solimano, A., (2002), "Crisis, Dollarization and Social Impact. The Case of Ecuador." *Directions in Development.* The World Bank (Forthcoming).

Eichengreen, B., (1996), *Globalizing Capital. A History of the International Monetary System.* Princeton University Press.

Krugman, P., (1979), "A Model of Balance of Payments Crises", *Journal of Money, Credit and Banking,* vol. 11, no.3, pp. 311-325.

Solimano, A., (1990), "Inflation and the Costs of Stabilization: Historical and Recent Experiences and Policy Lessons", *World Bank Research Observer* vol. 5, no. 2, pp. 167-85.

———— (1991), "The Economies of Central and Eastern Europe: An Historical and International Perspective" in V. Corbo, F. Coricelli and J. Bossak, ed., *Reforming Central and Eastern Europe: Initial Results and Challenges,* The World Bank.

III

UNDERSTANDING
THE IMPACTS OF THE CRISIS

6

CULTURE: NEW SPACES OF EXPRESSION?

NÉSTOR GARCÍA CANCLINI

When I was invited to address the topic, "New Spaces of Expression," I was struck by images of protests and demonstrations, interrupted by book stores permanently closing their doors, near-empty movie theaters, and turmoil in the streets combined with angry lines in front of banks and patient lines waiting at embassies. If, instead of this text, I had brought a video detailing these past weeks, we would hear the rumble of neighborhood meetings, anti-government protests, solitary voices passing through the Ezeiza airport, and millions of emails seeking job prospects as far away as Australia and New Zealand. I read about the resignation of Agustin Arteaga, Director of the newly inaugurated Latin American Art Museum in Buenos Aires, the first building in Argentina constructed solely to house a museum. Arteaga returned to Mexico because there would no longer be exhibitions on Lichtenstein, Diego Rivera, and Frida Kahlo; the backers of these exhibits pulled out after having to close some of their businesses.

1

Besides the oscillation between closed and open, new and old spaces, I find distinct modes of silence and expression, different manners of conceiving the country's place in the world and its current fall. One certainty is that this disintegration did not begin in December 2001. In this chapter, I will present a combination of some prior scenes with recent scenes, without pretending that they can be added together or used to arrive at a logical conclusion.

During the last week of August 2001, in a taxi in Buenos Aires, the driver quickly recounted the themes the whole country is discussing in newspapers and on television: economic despair has turned into social and political despair. Close to half the population will spoil their votes in the next election and already messages on the Internet propose write-in votes for comic strip characters on election day. Of those comic strip write-ins, the most votes went to a character named Clemente – "since he is drawn without hands, hopefully he won't be able to rob us."

"I already know who I am going to vote for," my taxi driver announced to me. "I'm going to put down José de San Martín...if I'm here."

"Where are you thinking of going?"

"I don't know yet. I prefer the United States, but this is a family plan. The twelve of us got together and the majority picked another country. I don't agree with this plan, but I think we would still be better off there than here."

"And there, will you still drive a taxi?"

"No. We are all going to start a business together."

"And if you invest, and then want to take out your money, do you think you will be able to?"

"We're talking about that. They are going to answer us this week. It seems like they will guarantee our money."

When we got out of the taxi, he confirmed what I had imagined about his destination, "If you are going near Varadero, and you want to eat good pasta, I will wait for you."

We may ask ourselves what is happening in Latin America? How can a country that had already expelled hundreds of thousands during the military dictatorships of the last decades continue to push Ecuadorians, Peruvians, and Colombians to move to Spain and Uruguayans to Australia, while others imagine that the United States and Cuba are comparable alternatives? This driver's family thought in August 2001, before the collapse, that their modest family investment would be safer on a Cuban beach than in Argentina. How did Argentina, the land that gave birth to Che Guevara, construct a vision of its invisibility and the conviction that a family can succeed if it goes to one or another of those northern destinations that have historically been regarded as disparately rival symbols? The familiar strategies of relocating oneself within the country or in the United States or Spain have been shaped for some time by parameters other than those that carry political-ideological divisions (Espinosa, 1998; Pedone, 2000 and 2001).

2

A document from the 1997 Andrés Bello Agreement, "Latin American Transformations and Perspectives of Integration," held that "current globalization is not wedded to any of the historic international utopias: religious universalism, bourgeois cosmopolitanism, or socialist or third-world internationalism."[1] Does this mark the end of the great stories? Today we know that the rubble of downtown Manhattan left behind thousands of deaths and a few resurrections. Amid the more striking of the latter, we again find solemn tales that the post-modern version of globalization has worked to bury. For example, the tale of Western civilization and its mission for all of humanity: of patriotism or of God and his many chosen peoples. In the face of the violent revival of these ancient stories, one wonders if these are the only resources left for preachers of the singular story of the all-knowing market and the integration of mankind through free trade. In fact, there exists a mix of narratives that hide their contradictions, for example that of the CIA that contracts terrorists and drug traffickers around the world and the businesses and transnational banks that make deals with thieving presidents and wait for them to pay their debts. In the end, we discover that the great thriller of neoliberal globalization is made with too many dangerous relations and impossible loves.

After the attack on New York, the loss of hundreds of thousands of jobs in hotels, restaurants, airlines, taxi companies, and other services reduced the fantasies of many Latin Americans of looking for a job in the United States. The half-empty airplanes that flew in the weeks following September 11 from Los Angeles, New York, Houston, and San Antonio returned to their countries young Mexicans, Salvadorians, and Guatemalans who didn't want to be drafted to fight in Islamic nations.

The exact opposite took place in June 2001. When no world war was in sight, seventy-two Argentine and

---

[1] Andrés Bello Agreement, p. 8.

Uruguayan soldiers arrived in Madrid, contracted by the Spanish army. This exercise was said to be one way of obtaining residence, lightening the steps required for those Spanish and Italian descendants who wait in line through the night at the embassies of these countries in Buenos Aires and Montevideo. Their grandparents had traveled from Europe to America fleeing wars; now, thousands of students of biotechnology, engineering, or the humanities were having discussions in the offices of Asturias and Galicia in Argentina. Six hundred passed exams in 2001 to leave Argentina for jobs paying $500 a month that do not await them in their own countries "even though you have a degree" – not even in the Spanish companies that now own the petroleum, natural gas, electricity, part of communications, and the publishing houses of various Latin American countries.

3

What effects has Argentina's model of modernization and integration had in its twenty years of application? To answer this we must evaluate its impacts on politics and economics as well as on socio-cultural development. Whereas classical liberalism postulated modernization for everyone, the neoliberal proposition brings selective modernization, going from the integration of societies to the submission of the population to elite Latin American businessmen, and of these to the transnational banks, investors, and creditors. Ample social sectors lose their employees and basic social securities, and the capacity for public action and sense of national purpose diminishes. For neoliberalism, exclusion is a component of modernization. Controlling inflation through adjustment policies and money obtained through privatization (of airlines, petroleum and mines, banks, state enterprises, and other branches) enabled the economies of some Latin American countries to revive or stabilize in the early 1990s. It was a fragile recovery, almost without improvements in employment, security, or health rates. It also failed to correct inequalities. The historic and structural disparity between and within countries became worse.

If we look at statistics from recent decades, Latin America seems a decaying continent. Even the countries most dynamic in other times — Argentina, Brazil, and Mexico — showed negative growth rates in the 1980s. National per capita income in the region decreased by 15%. The number of households below the poverty line rose from 5% in 1980 to 39% in 1990.[2] In Peru, where real production fell 10% during those years, social and economic collapse resumed, with the return of cholera, a 19th century plague. This disease reappeared in the 1990s in Bolivia, Argentina, Ecuador, and other countries. Argentine politicians prefer, however, to accuse Bolivian or Peruvian migrants for the reemergence of cholera and other "pre-modern" sicknesses like tuberculosis and measles, and for the increases in school dropout rates and urban violence. They would rather cast blame outside than admit these circumstances have more to do with the corruption and deficient vaccinations that accompany the decreased buying power of wages and the poverty that plagues 70% of the population.

Any temporary recovery limited to certain sectors of some countries will be precarious as long as external and internal debt is not renegotiated in a manner that permits

---

2 Nun, 2001 p. 289.

the sectors to grow together. The most destabilizing and impoverishing fact of the past thirty years is the suffocating increase of the external debt. Latin America owed $16 billion in 1970, $257 billion in 1980, and $750 billion in 2000. This last figure, according to calculations by ECLAC and SELA, is equivalent to 39% of the Gross Geographic Product and 201% of the region's exports. There is no possibility of reducing the more than 200 million poor, explains the Permanent Secretary of SELA, if we do not gather "the dispersed power of the debtors."[3]

Other aspects contribute to Argentina's slow modernization beyond the repetition of unequal exchanges between nations and empires. We find ourselves in the world as a group of nations with unstable governments, frequent military coup d'etats, and as suppliers of primary materials with declining prices. Our histories can be commercialized and converted into folk music and soap operas. We are an enormous mass of consumers for the manufacturers and technologies of the North, but we have low capacity to buy, paying off debts by selling our petroleum, banks, and airlines. As we are disconnecting ourselves from our heritage and the resources to manage, expand, and communicate it, our national and regional autonomy atrophies. The central tension is thus the following: We are left between the promises of cosmopolitan globalization and the loss of national plans.

Between the 1960s and 1980s, the creation of publishing houses in Argentina, Brazil, and Mexico produced "import substitution" in the field of literary culture that was instrumental in developing education and forming modern nations and democratic citizenries. In the last three

---

[3] Boyle, 2001.

decades, the majority of these publications have been bankrupted or sold to Spanish publishing houses, later bought by French, Italians, and Germans.

In Argentina, the transnationalization of communications began over ten years ago, delivering the majority of cultural industries to foreign companies. The returns offered for their investment carry no value in North American or European markets. Instead of contesting the foreign market for its products, Argentines – like Peruvians, Venezuelans, and Mexicans – prefer to become managers at Telefónica of Spain, AT&T, or CNN. Managers of local branches, however, are responsible for making profits for their bosses, not for making decisions. In the 1990s, decisions on the Latin American authors to be edited and published internationally moved from Buenos Aires and Mexico to Madrid and Barcelona. Now, even the decision of which authors from our countries we will be able to read is made in Madrid. The cultural supplement of the newspaper *Clarín* on March 16, 2002 was dedicated to "our foreign books." Because their Spanish editors cannot guarantee sales of at least 3,000 copies in Buenos Aires, the latest works of Arturo Carrera, Rodolfo Fogwill, César Aira, Clara Obligado, and Diana Bellessi will not be distributed in Argentina. Between the moment the books were contracted and the date of publication, the books were deemed unprofitable because of the economic collapse's effect on the purchasing power of Argentines. Thus, the conversation between the principal novelists and poets and their cultural audience is interrupted. At the end of the 1970s and beginning of the 1980s, the military dictatorship cut off dialogue between exiles with their compatriots: *The Buenos Aires Affair* (censored before the military assault by the government of Juan Domingo Perón), *Kiss of the Spider Woman* (1976), and hundreds of other books were not distributed in Argentina until democracy returned in 1983. Now, the authoritarianism of the market blocks knowledge even of those authors living in the country. In a cruel irony, the *Clarín* supplement published summaries of Aira and Fogwill's books, drawn up by Argentine critics living out of the country, with the books' prices in euros.

5

We spent the 1980s and 90s trying to globalize ourselves. Economists convinced politicians that they had to open their societies to foreign capital investment. The development of national industries ceased to matter. The decisive issue in evaluating a country became the number of investments attracted from various places and the number of products exported.

Our relation with the world seemed more important than the rooting of what was ours, as comunications hastened to bring us foreign movies from Hollywood, foreign television programs informing and entertaining us with their many choices, and music from regions previously known only to specialists. The latter began to be transmitted daily by radio to the smallest and most remote villages. Local culture became interesting only to those for whom the import-export market was no help: older generations more accustomed to domestic tastes, politicians with no knowledge of languages or unable to make transnational deals, local humanities professors, and nostalgic folklorists.

In these first months of the new century, the Latin American cinema and that of other regions are articulating the cosmopolitan with the local. Princess diaries, Himalayan tribes, captains' mandolins, and disembowelments are revisited. The new editions of Francis Coppola's *Apocalypse Now* and Steven Spielberg's *Jurassic Park* suggest that part of the film industry is unsure of how to speak about the present or recent past. To confuse or dazzle their audience each week, and allay their fear that the public will stay home, they return to shocking without exhibiting current uncertainties, to frightening with distant terrors.

The European and Latin American menu adds films that rework local pasts in order to return to thinking about daily fascism and social decay. Realizing that this decade began with films such as *Enemy Sweet Enemy* by Ettore Scola and *Broken Silence* by Montxo Armendáriz, we can ask if it is necessary to increase the enormous filmography about wars made since the mid-century. These creators, who have already contributed to the revision of persecutions under Mussolini and Franco, might answer that today's Europe needs to relearn the consequences of those experiences. In this respect, I prefer the ideas evoked by two Latin American movies, Lucrecia Martel's *The Swamp* and Barbet Schroeder's *Our Lady of the Assassins*, whose different themes point to a common idea: the current decadence of Latin America.

Aside from these films being valued as the best Argentine and Colombian films of recent years, *The Swamp* and *Our Lady of the Assassins* depict not only the past, but also our propensity to regress. This is achieved despite their concessions to a sense of humor that sells not only these films but also two other very enjoyable Argentine movies (*Nine Queens* and *The Son of the Bride*) as well as many energetic Mexican and Brazilian films.

Our Lady of the Assassins describes, with a dry language and without descending into bloody Tarantino-like scenes, the significance of violence without a state and the chaotic disintegration of social connections, blessed by religiosity. The protagonist returns to Colombia, to

Medellín to be exact, hoping to regain a sense of vitality among the destitution of his childhood. The film is set against a background of modernization in pieces, unable to eliminate symbolic and material misery in a city globalized by narco-traffickers that continues to use the local – the Virgin, local customs, and the language – to name and justify destruction.

The tragic humor of *The Swamp* sets the film on a horizon reiterating Magic Realism – natural violence, a storm, unbearable heat – but these elements are shown through a static story. We watch scenes in a pool that has been dirty for over three years, two houses whose inhabitants spend most of their time in bed, talking when no one is listening and screaming when others collapse. They drink wine and dye their hair. The "Indian" servant is the only character who helps the injured female owner of the house, and is the one accused of "stealing the towels and sheets." This strange Argentine film does not take place in Buenos Aires but rather in the northern province of Salta, near Bolivia, the poorest country in Latin America. The petite bourgeoisie of the film periodically dreams about taking a vacation in Bolivia; a few years earlier it would have proudly flown to Miami for a shopping trip.

Neither the shattered time of the murderous assassins nor the untamed time of the swamp is able to control the tensions between family and sex, work and unemployment, generational and ethnic gaps. Without throwing accusations and by expressing only the necessary, these films' return to Medellín and Salta are metaphors that go beyond the extreme national decay of Colombia and Argentina. Their lack of picturesque backgrounds and scenery conveys, with an unavoidable eloquence, a self destructive, broken continent.

Broken Silence by Montxo Armendáriz inspires reflection on Franco, fascism, and Latin American dictatorships.

The Spanish director relates the pain and misery of daily life in a small town in 1944-48. Fascism had already died in the rest of Europe, but the cruel authoritarianism continued in Spain, with guerillas hidden in mountains, aided by villagers who gave them food and information. Each time the police discover the villagers, a man loses a wife or a woman a husband. Even those who know that their relatives have escaped are subjected to indecencies, such as the young boy forced by an army sergeant to dig the grave in which his father will be buried once found. In the final scene, while the protagonist leaves her village after the assassination of her companion and her aunt, a quote by Bertolt Brecht appears on the screen: "In gloomy times, will we also sing? We will sing about the gloomy times."

This fight between cruelty and dignity under Franco traces parallels to the years after the dictatorship that were to free not only politics, but also daily life. The frivolous game of corrupt businesses aligned with the global destruction of a state of well-being and frequent returns to conservatism and discrimination, most noticeably xenophobia, have diluted hopes for democracy. Since this decay of historic experience is common in so many countries, the same question can be applied to the triumph of financial speculation over social necessities in other European and Latin American societies living under dictatorships: Is this where so much pain has led us?

Dwelling a moment on the experience of authoritarianism, one is shocked by the human capacity to be cruel or indifferent towards those who dare to break the silence. From a long-range perspective, the failure to learn from collective periods of suffering is shocking. How can we not connect recent social and economic failures with the difficulty in judging the assassins? In Argentina, the leaders of the military junta were condemned to prison sentences that were shortened by amnesty decrees and a law of "due obedience." In Spain, Brazil, Guatemala, and Uruguay, those found guilty of torture, execution, kidnapping, and disappearances were never prosecuted. Chile permitted its criminals to continue living on the same streets as their victims, raising them to political positions and expanding their authority until the tenacity of a Spanish judge and the rather inconsistent English justice system put an unavoidable reversal to the eighteen sinister years of Augusto Pinochet.

The majority of politicians, businessmen, union leaders, and communicators prefer to forget these tragedies and marginalize those who remind others that human rights in the present depend on the occurrences of the past. They do not want anything to separate them from quick profits. For personal gain and advantage, they make agreements with violators and perpetrators, willing to return to them — even in democratic times — a degree of control over former victims. Military and police officers, with obedient ministers and civil servants, destroyed the social fabric during the military dictatorships. Afterwards, political, economic, and social leaders contributed to despotism through their own amnesia. Retired from the government, their detrimental effects on society continued. Through the repeated economic misfortune that has taken its toll on a majority of lives (even in countries with successful microeconomic indicators like Spain and Chile), virtually the only lasting legacy is disenchantment.

What can be sung about when we forget the gloomy times? Music, literature, and cinema can speak of the forgotten and the recurrence of dark times. If films are able to echo in the public and to sell well internationally, like *The Swamp* and *Our Lady of the Assassins*, they reveal something in the middle of the decadence. Culture, song, and film make sense and not only for us, it seems; *New York Times* critic Ruby Rich called *The Swamp* a film that helped to change U.S. conceptions of Latin America and the relationship between Latin and Hollywood cinema. This may be too much responsibility for one movie, especially when the collapse bears the potential for so many more projects.

6

What happens to cultures that lose their local character to globalization? They not only lose social and economic strength, but also significance. I find no more eloquent description of this than the story *The Last Train in Jujuy* by Héctor Tizón, which refers to the "border lands" of Northern Argentina with Bolivia. "In this country," he says, "only an aging man can remember the times when we belonged to the First World." According to Tizón, in his childhood, the greatest characteristic of this part of Argentina was its railways. He says that his teacher in Yala

> – one of the last male teachers in this region – would repeat and make us copy in our notebooks: in 1870, 700 kilometers; in 1892, 13,000 kilometers; in 1916, 34,000 kilometers; in 1946, over 40,000 kilometers. This information was for us, the children of this land, much like familiar statistics of patriotic wars, like the beloved headstones in the cemeteries, like the crumbling documents in family coffers.

It was a time when the local made sense as part of the nation, when there was a will to connect these regions and integrate them through transportation and communications. The trains Tizón evokes united the regions of the country and gave them their place in the world. In this way, they are reminiscent of the "special car of Luis Angel Firpo, after his memorable feat of arriving in the north for his unforgettable Homeric exhibitions," or the memory of Josip Broz, later Tito, "shepherd, waiter, iron worker, who between 1920 and 1929 emigrated to Argentina and worked on the construction of the Huaytuquina railway in Salta." "I met an old prostitute, later a respectable matron, who asserted with undeniable proof, to have been the great love of the railway worker, who much later became 'emperor' of Yugoslavia." This description shows us the pre-global local produced in interaction with national and international contexts. Even in early periods of modernity, in regions beyond the port of Buenos Aires the local did not exist within itself. The cultural and economic way of life of the village in Jujuy was made possible through the extension of a national means of transportation, sports, and cultural and political figures from distant regions.

Tizón writes in his description of the 1980 trip of the last train to reach Jujuy:

> My house was not far from the rail tracks that, for over a century, carried passengers towards Bolivia. From there, I heard a train that hardly halted in passing and I knew it would be one of the last. Post-modernity had arrived to these lands as well. I struggled through the thin eucalyptus forest that separated the confines of my house from the tracks. I stood on the border of their land, next to the gaucho Demetrio Hernández who has recently died and whose story I will tell in another chapter.
>
> The sun is setting. It's nearly night and the train carries a dozen semi-illuminated wagons full of indigenous migrants making their way to the border. I say nothing. The gaucho Hernández says, just to say it,

"It stops for nothing. It doesn't even take on water anymore as it used to." Then I speak, only to break the silence, "They say it won't pass by anymore." He looks at me. "Because of the progress of the First World," I say. Then he says, "I've heard about that." "Is progress the same as death, Don Hernández?" I ask. As the last train pulls out he answers: "No. Progress doesn't mean anything."

This desolate isolation, from a lack of railways or other resources or means of communications, is occurring more frequently in Latin America. Such a landscape should form part of the international theoretical debate on whether globalization is similar to imperialism, is disguised Americanization, or is "glocal". In other words, on what remains of the local, what has been mixed together, is elsewhere, or is no longer anywhere.

Faced with the dismantling of local projects, an end to industrialization, and the isolation of many regions, some believe their only options for development are to side with globalization or to defend the local. I think rather, that we need to construct more democratic options that are more equitably distributed so that we may all have access to the local and the global, to combine as we wish.

Denationalization and de-globalization have modified the character and agendas of opposition movements as well. With the preponderance of so many forms of plunder and disconnection, the actors and themes of protests are multiplying. One study[4] of the popular protests and *cacerolazos* in Argentina at the end of 2001 asked the participants, "Why did you come?" Many participants answered,

---

[4] Fernández, Borakievich, and Rivera, 2002.

"I have nothing to lose." The difference is that these people now belong to more heterogeneous social sectors than those that protested previously. In the classic socialist movements, those who had nothing to lose were the workers, in Peronism the "people" or the "shirtless." The study observed that in recent weeks, those joining the protests had lost work, managed to keep their jobs but lost part of their wages, lost their pension, housing, or profession, and/or had their savings confiscated by the banks, and "also lost their future and their dignity." Another common phrase is, "I'm here for the future of my children." With different levels of spiritual and material need, joining the protests are "the always poor, the new poor, and the future poor."

Although it is still early to tell what will come of these protests and fragile organizations composed outside of and far from political parties, they are changing the perception of those disenchanted with politics. There is de-partisanization, which we can no longer confuse with de-politicization.

7

The 1980s have been called the lost decade in Latin America because of the region's zero growth. How then shall we label the 1990s? Among other things it was the decade of impunity: of the appropriation of Latin American heritage by transnational corporations and governments that privatized even profitable companies, under the pretext that some state enterprises were not profitable. Economic supports were emptied and local working conditions destroyed, thus diminishing the possibility of participating competitively and with dignity in the international arena.

I do not wish to issue a hurried prognosis of this first decade of the new century. We do not know where the protests and conflicts will lead. They have already brought too many deaths to deem them transformative powers; their efficacy will be evaluated on their ability to come up with alternative sociopolitical and economic programs.

One novelty that has arisen in these first months of the 20th century is the reopening of questions — for example, on the viability of a capitalism that expands its profits by aligning its financial operations with drug traffickers, the weapons industry, and corrupt politicians. Questions in Latin America, Europe, and the United States are opening up concerning the place of productivity in economic growth, of work in national productivity, and of nation-states and the globalization of the economy, technologies, and culture. The impunity of alarming business practices and the single-minded mentality that "authorized" them is starting to decline.

This is not the best period to write about Latin American integration. Yet exploring its potential in view of our own cultural practices can help us to imagine a globalization more sustainable than products, more lasting than opportunistic investors. As "content production" gains a space among cultural industries, many Latin Americans make themselves seen and read to renovate their repertories and narrative styles. Soap operas, ethnic music, urban cinema, and experimental literature show how to explore new spaces for cultures that do not speak English.

This implies that we will save ourselves through culture. It is necessary to write "culture" in lower case, just as the descriptions of "Argentine" or "Latin American" in Spanish are written in lower case, compared to "Military Alliances" or "Politics," words that in these warlike times are written in Spanish with capital letters. We must mark the difference between so many words that were used to solemnize the past. "National" or "Latin American" can grow if we nourish them with open, renewed, and united exchanges. To interpolate this name, "Latin American," in the global dialogue, and find the correct way to write it is what we must aim toward, so that our identity is not read between quotation marks.

The poet Juan Gelman, who writes entirely in the lower case, asks where we can find a home for those who had to move "elsewhere with the defeat." He answers, "our only right is to begin once again." Agreed – but it is worth pointing out that we are not starting from zero. We Latin Americans already have a place co-producing and communicating through film and the recordings we make, or are waiting to make while searching for a television that will represent us. We know we must do more than increase our sales and exports. As I listen to Astor Piazzola interpreted by Di Meola, and on other recordings by Gerry Mulligan, Gary Burton, and Gidon Kremer, I realize these facts are only significant if they serve the conversation we are having with the world. Our current position derives from our capacity to learn from memory and conversations with others. The Social Forum of Porto Alegre has become worldwide and is held simultaneously and teleconferenced with the World Economic Forum. Pedro Almodóvar listened to Chavela Vargas. Ry Cooder listened to the Buena Vista Social Club and Wim Wenders realized that he needed to film them.

To look for another place is sometimes to find nothing more than promises. It is to be assaulted in new lands by powers other than those that protect the same unedited and illiterate laws that we learned in our own market. It is to describe our fantasies and plans before stumbling into thieves or media eager to convert the latest assault into a reality show. It is to imagine culture as a story, impending but not yet occurring, as a crash that may still be avoided. It is to describe the possible experience of others. It is to rely on others.

8

Scenes from a dream. Pieces of a country that spent years without waking and celebrated, with doubtful and fragile joy, the recovery of democracy. A country that uses its memory and the rest of its energy to walk, trips without actually falling, so that the movement becomes neither an action nor a dream. The new spaces of expression still aren't new public scenes. Lines, demonstrations, protests, escapes.

New spaces for expression? Argentina now finds itself with an interrupted neoliberal program in which entire sectors are excluded from productivity or consumption. Unable to find representation among the politicians or voices in the government, they block roads and confront people in the streets in *escraches* (i. e. public denunciations). One innovation in recent months is that public demonstrations that previously took place in front of the homes of amnestied torturers are now extending to those of all politicians. Just as people's compulsive consumerism shows itself every few minutes in the movies, the eruption of unsatisfied sectoral interests repeatedly interrupts the story of globalization.

Recent cultural and anthropological studies have shown that most of the recent political voices do not aspire to obtain power or to control the state. Toward what goal did the Chinese students display their "immeasurable courage" when challenging the tanks in Tiananmen Square, asks

Craig Calhoun, if it was obvious beforehand that they would fail? The functional mode of thinking that concerns itself with interest and is solely aware of the rationality of economic and macro-political success is unable to understand action that strives to legitimize or express ideas. These are, says Calhoun, "fights for significance."[5]

The expression *aparición con vida*, "appearance alive" – still used by mothers of the disappeared – does not imply that they are waiting to find their children alive, just as the expression *que se vayan todos*, "get rid of all of them," should not be interpreted literally. Rather,

> its evocative power rests precisely in what its lack of viability makes manifest. They attack employing politics conceived as the art of the possible and show both the exhaustion of those forms of politics and the radical nature of those which should be invented collectively. Everyone who sings and hears them amid an emptiness of meaning and action not only denounces but also appeals for the invention of new meanings, the initiation of new forms of action.[6]

In examining the solidarity and group cohesion dimensions of these cultural and social practices, one sees political actions that do not seek direct fulfillment of demands or commercial interests but rather claim the structures of meaning of certain modes of life. Nevertheless, these acts – even when their successes arise from taking hold of silences and contradictions of the hegemonic order – fail to quench the question of how to arrive at a general reconfiguration of politics.

---

[5] Calhoun, 1992.

[6] Fernández et al.

References

Andrés Bello Agreement, (1997), *Programa: pensamiento renovado de integración. Seminario: "Las transformaciones de América Latina y las perspectivas de la integración"*, Santiago de Chile, May 5-6.

Andrés Bello Agreement and the Cultural Ministry of Colombia, (1999), *Economía & Cultura. Un estudio sobre el aporte de las industrias culturales y del entretenimiento al desempeño económico de los países de la Comunidad Andina. Informe preliminar. Definiciones básicas, pautas metodológicas y primeros resultados en Colombia*, Bogotá, November.

Boye, Otto, (2001), "Los acuerdos regionales para la deuda externa en América Latina y el Caribe", Conference on the Social Debt, organized by the Latin American Parliament and held in Caracas, Venezuela from July 10-13, 2001. http://lanic.utexas.edu/~sela /AA2K1/ ESP/ponen/ponen20.html

Calhoun, Craig, (1992), "The Infrastructure of Modernity: Indirect Social Relationships, Information Technology and Social Integration" in H. Haferkamp and N.J. Smelser, eds., *Social Change in Modernity*. Berkeley: University of California Press.

———— (1999), "El problema de la identidad en la acción colectiva" in Javier Auyero, *Caja de herramientas*, Buenos Aires, Universidad Nacional de Quilmes.

Espinosa, Víctor, (1998), *El dilema del retorno. Migración, género y pertenencia en un contexto transnacional*, México, El Colegio de Michoacán-El Colegio de Jalisco.

Fernández, Ana María, Sandra Borakievich and Laura B. Rivera, (2002), "La importancia de pedir lo posible", *Página 12*, Buenos Aires, March 14. http://pagina12.feedb.../index.php?id

Gelman, Juan, (1993), *En abierta oscuridad*, México, Siglo XXI.

Nun, José (2001), *Marginalidad y exclusión social*, México, FCE.

Pedone, Claudia, (2000), "Globalización y migraciones internacionales. Trayectorias y estrategias migratorias de ecuatorianos en Murcia, España" in *Scripta Nova. Revista Electrónica de Geografía y Ciencias Sociales*, Universidad de Barcelona, vol. 69 N° 49, August.

———— (2001), "La 'otra' mirada desde mi condición de inmigrante extracomunitaria. Comentarios al artículo de Horacio Capel, *Inmigrantes en España*". http://www.ub.es/geocrit/sn-85.html

7

The Crisis and the Social Question in Argentina: Notes for the Debate

Adriana Clemente

The main objective of this chapter is to put forth a group of preliminary observations on the current Argentine social situation, in light of the worsening economic and political crisis that triggered the social upheaval and popular mobilization of December 2001. In this context, I propose as a member of the International Institute for the Environment and Development, Latin America (IIED-LA), as part of the non-governmental sector, to reflect on the "social question" in Argentina, identifying, with hindsight, the evolution of those social and economic indicators that have signaled the evolution and orientation of public social spending. The second part of this chapter will share critical observations on the profile and the claims of social policies implemented in the framework of state reform. Finally, it will analyze the behavior of nongovernmental groups and new social actors in the acute reassessment of the state's role as principle actor for public good.

THE SOCIAL QUESTION IN ARGENTINA

The social question concerns the mass of excluded people, abandoned by the irrational application of a given economic model. In this model, the state favored the interests of the political class and the logic of the market over guarantees of citizens' rights and the public good. Unemployment, poverty, and corruption are some of the problems that can be seen as isolated phenomena or as a "social question" that Argentine society will have to analyze in order to avoid the disintegration of society.[1]

In the past decade, while the majority of countries in the region have decreased the percentage of their populations living in poverty, Argentina has worsened considerably, increasing from 7% in 1986 to 19% in 1996 (UNDP, 1999). Because of the economic recession of the past four years, the National Institute of Statistics and Census (INDEC – *Instituto Nacional de Estadística y Censos*) estimates that approximately 40% of the population is now living in poverty.

Paradoxically, in 1999, Argentina was among the 45 countries with the highest index of human development, according to the UN. This ranking includes various indicators, such as life expectancy, which in Argentina is calculated to be 72.9 year; literacy, estimated at 96.5%; and per capita GDP, which was $10,300 in 1997. Argentina was second in Latin America only to Chile, which was ranked 34th worldwide. Currently, according

---

[1] In this chapter, "social question" refers to R. Castell's definition (1997), as the hiatus between the political organization and the economic system. The "social" area links both without strictly following either economic or political logic. The social question is a concept in which a society tests the ambiguities of its cohesion and tries to avoid its risk of fracture.

to a study based on United Nations data, per capita income has decreased by 64.8% since 1997, placing Argentina below Uruguay, Chile, Brazil, Mexico, and Venezuela in the ranking. This abrupt fall requires us to see the relativity of the statistics, particularly GDP indicators, if not related to other variables such as distribution of earnings.

THE EVOLUTION OF POVERTY AND THE DISTRIBUTIVE VARIABLE

Argentina's recorded income distribution is currently at its worst since measurements began in the 1970s. In Central and Greater Buenos Aires (where nearly 30% of the national population lives), in October 2001 – before the events of December – the richest 10% of the population received 37.3% of total income. Conversely, the poorest 10% received only 1.3%. Estimates in January 2002 calculate that unemployment for this region went from 14.7% in 2001 to 23.8% in 2002. Furthermore, 3.7 million people came to live in poverty, 80% of these coming from the urban middle class. This will be a decisive indicator in the worsening of these results in future measurements.[2]

Projecting these 2001 figures to the national level, it is estimated that the wealthy received 28.7 times as much as the poor. In 1974, the gap was 12.3 times. This increase signifies the transfer of wealth from those sectors with the

---

[2] *Clarín*, March 31, 2002.

least resources to the highest strata of society. The hyper-inflation of the 1980s and the recession and unemployment of the 1990s have widened this gap, which now seems irreversible.

The neoliberal model, applied in its most orthodox form in Argentina, found one of its most representative expressions in two policies: privatization and labor flexibility. It is necessary to briefly review the application and visible consequences of these policies in order to understand the failure of the model and its role in generating poverty, exclusion, and corruption.

The privatization of state enterprises originally found favor in public opinion under two premises: A promise to invest in areas such as health, education, and security, and an improvement in the quality, coverage, and cost of public services.[3] In both aspects, the results were disappointing. As far as improving and increasing the application of public spending, although privatizations represented $18 billion in state earnings between 1990 and 1998, this money was largely used early in the convertibility period to shrink the fiscal deficit. In the mid- and long run, the policies produced a $20 billion dollar debt for businesses. As for social spending, payment of provincial debts was the major expenditure. Looking at the relation of public enterprise privatizations and its negative impact on the labor market, it is estimated that public service enterprises decreased their workforce by 70% between 1995 and 1998.

---

[3] The State Reform Law (23,696) and the Economic Emergency Law (23,697) provided the political and legal frameworks for 80 percent of the privatizations that took place in less than five years. Both laws were responses to the defeat of the Radical Party in the 1989 presidential

Two of the principal negative consequences of the adjustment programs in the region have been unemployment and underemployment. A study conducted by the Economic Commission for Latin America and the Caribbean (ECLAC, 1990) found that in fifteen Latin American countries, urban unemployment was greater in 1990 than in the previous decade. In Argentina, this was criticized as early as the mid-1990s. It reached as high as 18% of the economically active population in 1996 and rose above 20% in official measurements conducted in February 2002. Labor statistics are equally disheartening. At the beginning of the 1990s, illegal employment represented 25% of the economically active population while in 2001 it was estimated at 38.6%. The following table shows the negative evolution of this indicator.

EVOLUTION OF UNEMPLOYMENT (IN PERCENTAGES)

1981	1982	1983	1984	1985	1986	1987	1988	1989	1990
5.4	4.6	3.9	4.4	5.9	5.2	5.7	6.1	7.1	6.3

1991	1992	1993	1994	1995	1996	1997	1998	1999	2000
6.0	7.0	9.3	12.2	16.6	17.3	13.7	12.4	13.8	14.7

Source: Permanent Survey of Households, INDEC

---

elections and to the conditions that forced then president-elect, Carlos Menem, to take office early and with a free hand in state reform matters.

EXTERNAL DEBT AND SOCIAL DEBT

The external debt in Argentina has an inversely proportional relationship to the country's development. From the beginning of the dictatorship in March 1976 to the year 2001, the debt multiplied nearly twenty times, from less than $8 billion to around $160 billion. In the same period, Argentina reimbursed lenders by around $200 billion, or around twenty-five times what it owed in March 1976. According to a 1986 UNDP report, it is estimated that Latin America spends around one third of its export earnings to service its debt. In the case of Argentina, these payments largely reflect the extent of its mounting debts. The IMF loan in negotiation since the events of December 2001 is an example: approximately 60% of the requested loan will go to pay the next installments of the current debt.

GROWTH OF THE EXTERNAL DEBT

Year	Debt
	(in millions of US$)
1976	9,739
1980	27,162
1983	45,069
1989	62,843
1994	90,094
1997	129,100
1999	147,881

Note: Service Paid 1976-2000: US$ 212,280,000

THE INFLUENCE OF MULTILATERAL COOPERATION ON SOCIAL POLICIES

According to a 2000 World Bank report[4], Argentina had one of the highest indices of social sector spending, as a percentage of GDP (17.6%) and in terms of absolute value ($1,594 per year per inhabitant). Based on these figures, we can say that during the convertibility period, Argentina was closer to OECD countries than to many of its Latin American neighbors. Nevertheless, these figures mask profound signs of poverty induced by poor distribution of national resources and public resources.

The composition of spending makes the redistribution of resources within the social sector more difficult. Almost half of social spending (48%) is controlled by the provincial and municipal governments; 32% is reserved for the government-run pension system; and the major part of the remaining 20% finances basic sectoral programs like primary education and health services. Specific national social program spending comes to a total of merely 3.5% of total social sector spending, representing 0.6% of GDP.[5] The following graph exhibits the inadequate composition of public social spending.

---

[4] World Bank. *Poor People in a Rich Country*, Report No. 19992-AR, Buenos Aires, March 2000.

[5] According to World Bank estimates, social expenditure has improved slightly. Twenty-two percent of total social expenditure reaches the poorest fifth of the population while 19 percent reaches the richest fifth (World Bank, 1999). The public service infrastructure (drinking water, sewage systems, etc.) is concentrated mostly in Buenos Aires and other major urban areas.

DISTRIBUTION OF SOCIAL SPENDING

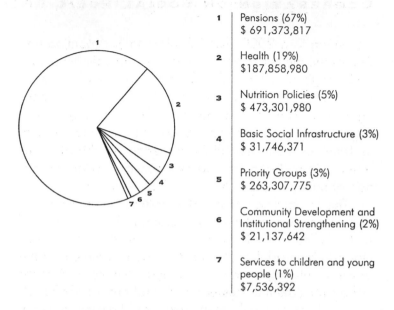

1	Pensions (67%)	$ 691,373,817
2	Health (19%)	$187,858,980
3	Nutrition Policies (5%)	$ 473,301,980
4	Basic Social Infrastructure (3%)	$ 31,746,371
5	Priority Groups (3%)	$ 263,307,775
6	Community Development and Institutional Strengthening (2%)	$ 21,137,642
7	Services to children and young people (1%)	$7,536,392

Source: Based on SIEMPRO data, 2000. Amounts accrued until 31/12/2000 by the social programs of the MDSyMA.

In Argentina, multilateral development banks have directed their efforts towards influencing health reform, the labor market, and the state through credits. A 1999 study on the nature of multilateral cooperation indicates that World Bank operations in Argentina had then grown to 44 projects at a cost of nearly $6.9 billion. Similarly, the Inter-American Development Bank (IDB) had 26 projects underway in 1997 at a cost of $4.4 billion.[6]

---

[6] *Multilateral Cooperation in Argentina 1997/1999.* United Nations, Argentina.

In the case of the IDB, 30% of the loan portfolio reaches areas of Public Sector Spending (PSS) encompassing education, urban development, health, and science; another 31% goes to provincial reforms and provincial banks; while only 8% goes for credit to small- and mid-sized producers. This reveals the emphasis the IDB places on the reform and modernization process.[7]

In the case of the World Bank, 27% of resources are designated to areas associated with PSS. Out of that total, 42% goes toward reforming temporary systems (transfers from provincial banks) and social work. In this sense, these resources cannot be considered an increase in spending in terms of monetary transfers to beneficiaries.

The contribution of multilateral development banks is slight: In 1999, they contributed a total of 4-5% of total PSS. The strategic orientation of the resources contributed by the multilateral development banks to influence the PSS can best be seen in the areas where credit is concentrated. For example, the portion of resources allocated to "state modernization" corresponds to the potential for governments to influence the efficacy of the PSS, in programs focusing on health, education, and emergency employment. In each of these cases, they are designed toward improving the population's social well-being as measured by the NBI, *Necesidades Básicas Insatisfechas*, an index of "unsatisfied basic needs."

Among the undesired results of a political sector influenced by multilateral development banks is the fragmentation of benefits and problems, the consequences of

---

[7] The Inter-American Development Bank provides 1 billion pesos for state reform in the provinces; World Bank funds dedicated to provincial state reform total US $230 million. *Multilateral Cooperation 1997/99.*

which are observed in the Social Development Ministry. In the last two years, this ministry has been working to implement over 60 programs in areas where it found deficiencies in aid disbursement and targeting. Municipal governments have shown they are better organized to implement programs designed to focus on families versus individuals. Evaluations by INDEC completed in 1999 showed deficiencies in social program coverage. Problems of access and the balance between supply and demand bring additional difficulties to the programs that – in spite of their compensatory goals – are not able to cover structural discrepancies, such as nutrition and sanitation, in the poorest sectors.

In confronting the crisis, direct assistance must shift material from the focused to the universal. This could be read as a step backwards in the modernization discourse of the multilateral development banks on the "spillover theory," *teoria del derrame*, which suggests that while recipients are awaiting the benefits of the model only the weakest of the weak need to be protected. Currently in Argentina, however, due to the irrational application of both state restructuring and the economic system, political stability and the ability of families to feed themselves are threatened.

In response to the emergency, the national government is trying to pay a US$ 50 subsidy to the heads of 1.2 million unemployed families. As of December 2001, with more than 20% of the economically active portion of the population unemployed, this subsidy reached only 150,000 heads of households. The suspension of these meager resources and the rupture of the chain of supply were among other motives that unleashed the events of December, particularly those affecting the poorest classes.

CRISIS AND SOCIAL PARTICIPATION

In recent years, new social organizations aimed to promote social participation and consolidate the institutional performance of community social organizations and NGOs. They tried either to execute programs, reducing operating costs, while increasing the impact of social intervention, or to increase control over expenses. Whatever the intention, in recent years, one of these motivations managed to facilitate dialogue between the governmental and non-governmental sectors at the level of social policies.

Before December, public participation was a phenomenon restricted to public meetings organized by non-governmental or governmental – mainly local government – organizations. The many popular protests of recent months, however, do not resemble these previously organized meetings. Rather, and in spite of their heterogeneous character, they can be grouped into three categories, according to their objectives for participation: reclaiming rights, meeting needs, and network management and democratic participation.

We can further describe each of these categories. *Reclaiming rights* refers to a questioning of the established order through street mobilization and protest without the organized structure of a political party, including picketing and cutting off major roadways, and the many variations of street protests known in Argentina as *cacerolazos* and *escraches*. *Meeting needs* refers to the phenomenon whereby individuals have joined to create new circuits for providing necessities and provisions through tactics such as barter fairs, networks of direct assistance and voluntary mutual aid. *Network management and democratic participation* refers to sectoral or territorial associations that grew up around a demand for resolution to social problems. Of the three, these latter most closely came out of social programs. The low degree of visibility received by this institutionalized form of public-private association can be attributed to its high degree of separation from politics, a sphere that is being severely questioned at this moment.[8]

Network management can be sustained when at least one of the participating parties is capable of investing, particularly if that party is representative of the government. The possibility of additional investment in these networks is what differentiates protest from self-management. With the crumbling of the government's promotion and regulation of public well-being, we observe a proliferation of organized mechanisms characterized by both associations and a politicizing of social participation.

People created a new significance for the formal spaces for democratic participation: they protested at the Congress and Plaza de Mayo, they debated in the squares, they organized street marches. Popular protests in these recent months led to a questioning of investments in induced social promotion. This remains the principal challenge for promoters of social participation.

THE SOCIAL AGENDA AND THE CRISIS

Non-governmental organizations offer a new option for direct assistance in cases where a failure of direct assistance to meet demand is a principal motivation for social

---

[8] This classification does not claim to be a typology and instead constitutes a kind of classification for a primary description of the configuration of associations emerging from the crisis.

conflict. In this sense, the national social agenda should consider two assistance plans: one for emergencies to provide quick answers on questions of subsistence needs; and a second, to attempt to mitigate and repair previous damage. For example, the infrastructure that the state tried to dissolve in these years needs to be reinvented. In this vein, the coverage and quality of the social network will be the principal challenge.

The central point for reconstruction of the political social agenda at both the governmental and non-governmental level could be:
• *Territoriality:* This refers to the local level acting as protagonist in resolving problems and as a factor of social cohesion.
• *Citizenship:* Dignifying the beneficiary of emergency loans.
• *Generating Income:* Promoting a combination of direct assistance programs with income earning incentives from a social economic perspective.
• *Network Management:* Deepening and politicizing the model of network management, working in an alliance of democratic governance.

The challenge for non-governmental organizations is to regain the focus of the protests without losing the benefits of association between governmental and non-governmental groups. In this sense, a deepening of relations with local governments is a valid aim, particularly because results are easily seen at this level. In this framework, we propose that NGOs remain active in necessary and strategic issues such as: access to privatized public services, ownership of land and decent housing, and employment through socio-economic initiatives. At the same time, work should be done on the viability of micro-regional economies and those initiatives that generate jobs and income. In this regard, work between NGOs, local governments, and the social leadership is an indispensable strategy.

Organizations in the nongovernmental sector that focus on development must seek out mechanisms for influencing public politics that are more effective. Such measures could include designing intervention proposals with sectors living in poverty that are searching for a combination of three key components: a recovery of lost rights, a hierarchical ordering of social capital, and income earning opportunities. In a state of emergency, the support and consolidation of the types of organizations discussed above is acutely strategic.

This perspective of facing social issues though integration requires a critical revision of the assumptions around which the nongovernmental sector has worked in recent years. This emergency, as in all cases of emergency, calls for a review of theories and practices. At this moment, all of society is engaged in this critical and hopeful effort.

REFERENCES

Abeles, Martín, (1999), *La privatización de los servicios públicos básicos y su impacto en los sectores populares*, FLACSO Economy and Technology Area.

Aglamisis, Jorgelina, (2001), "Soy demasiado viejo para conseguir trabajo y demasiado joven para morirme", in *Ciencias Sociales* N° 47. Publication of the School of Social Sciences, University of Buenos Aires.

Information Bulletin of the Observatory of Trasnationals, (2002), *Analysis of the Argentine External Debt.*

Castells, Robert, (1997), *La metamorfosis de la cuestión social,* Paidós: Buenos Aires.

United Nations Argentina, *Multilateral Cooperation in Argentina, 1997-99.*

SIEMPRO (System of Monitoring and Evaluation of Social Programs), (2000), *Informe de Políticas y Programas Sociales.* N° 2.

UNDP, (1999), Human Development Report.

World Bank, (2000), *Poor People in a Rich Country,* Report N° 1999-AR, Buenos Aires.

8

POLITICAL DIMENSIONS
OF THE CRISIS

ERNESTO SEMÁN

The task of looking at the "The political issues of the transition" implies two optimistic assumptions. First, that Argentina is actually in a transition, effectively going from one point to another; that we are at a moment of history as described by Marx and quoted many times, when the old world has not yet finished dying and the new one has not quite been born. Besides being optimistic, it is an assumption that helps put aside some of the debates now abounding in Argentina, about the "real sense" or the "unique meaning" of the *piquetes* and *cacerolazos*, referring to the protests, riots, and lootings. These have been described by the media, intellectuals, and politicians as anti-political movements, middle class-interest protest, a new way of politics, an expression of the breakdown of the classic social protest. What they really are is something incomplete; as part of this transition, they are facts in a founding moment itself, its meaning still being built and still unknown.

The other optimistic assumption is that not only economic but also political issues are currently under discussion in deciding the possible "technical solutions" to move on from the crisis. How big, how biased, and how ideological are the limits of the economic debate imposed and slipped into this "technical knowledge" about the options available? The economic restrictions are real and clearly exist — to deny them would be a crime. To disregard the social and political restrictions as well is also a crime and a technical mistake, as they have now emerged as strongly as economic restrictions. To say there are "political issues" in the transition admits this is a normative debate, not just a technical one. It also implies there is a discussion being held on how a group of people and ideas are able to lead the country and the limits, economic and otherwise, of this leadership.

Having said that, I would like to discuss three facts, ideas, or levels that the crisis calls into question, although surely with different results, coming from each one of these levels. First, and most general, is the lack of a development model in Argentina since at least the 1970s, when the export of commodities and import-substitution industrustrialization had clearly reached a level of exhaustion. The model was no longer able to guarantee with proper resources what it had provided for decades: a country with social mobility, that was relatively modern and somewhat developed, with an active social and cultural life. These aspects marked Argentina as uniquely different from the general Latin American pattern. It is in this lack of a national development plan that we find one of the few and saddest continuities from the last dictatorship to the democratic state.

The sociologist Alain Touraine has blamed Argentina's crisis on a lack of a national elite that is ready and able to design a national project. Touraine also argues that

"Argentines" – certainly a vague category, I would say – have always built their identity in relation to the international cultural movement, never laying out their own project according to their own expectations. From Paris, he recently said that Argentina is a country that just does not exist anymore, because it is a country of consumption, not a country of work and production.

It is hard to deny such a claim in light of the crisis, but some shadings need to be pointed out. We could say, as did historian Tulio Halperín Donghi, that the lack of a national perspective – if such a thing really exists – has been noticeable since the 1970s, and that the hyperinflation of 1989 put an end to an active and egalitarian *Argentina Peronista*. It would be interesting, however, to go over that breaking point again and review how Menem's arrival in office changed those old patterns, in light of current circumstances.

Because the departure points of Menemism from the "old Argentina" were so large, so drastic, and so dramatic – even visually – all our concentration has remained focused on them, while other patterns of equal or greater importance continued to rule the country's development. Beside the impact of the changes, something else postponed the debate about what things remained the same. It was the idea that the first democratic government had come to restore democratic institutions, the second gave us economic stability, and the third, with De la Rúa, would basically bring everything else and fix the problems left from the other two administrations: it would reduce the social gap and it would clean corruption out of the institutions. Thus, we had to wait through the entire period to learn the final outcome.

As is evident, the third government did not take care of everything else – it actually did little or nothing. Further, its failure unintentionally demonstrated that democratic institutions had not been useful enough as a framework to allow or encourage political and economic actors to design a new development project. In the end, the old idea that Argentina was a "rich" country that only had to bring itself into accord with new international ideas proved to be a theme that continued through Argentine politics during the 1990s.

Perhaps that is why we have already "celebrated" or "commemorated" the death of the old Argentina at least three times in the last 20 years: in 1983, 1989, and now. Thus, the notion of an Argentina characterized by social mobility and relative egalitarianism resembles less a death, than a missing person. It is something we mourn every now and then in the face of the evidence of its absence, which does not say as much about its strength and durability, as about the lack of a suffcent replacement.

The second level that the crisis questions is democracy itself: its place and effectiveness in this process. After almost nineteen years of democracy, it has been the framework and scenario of a long process of institutional deterioration, social exclusion, and growing inequality. After nineteen years of political democracy, Argentina is not much more of a a democratic society now than in 1983.

Today we see the collapse of the political system, yet that this has not implied, until now, the collapse of the political regime is a miracle, based on an extraordinary democratic conviction among Argentines. The occasional rumours of a potential coup d'état remind me of the debates in New York City after September 11, when some asked, "Why did the towers fall? Why didn't they remain standing?" What is shocking is not that they fell, but that they took so much time to do it, after being hit by two planes. Similar questions could be asked about Argentine democracy today. One of the founding ideas of the restored democracy in 1983 was its extension to social life, craftily expressed by Raúl Alfonsín in his campaign with the motto: *"Con la democracia se come, se cura, se educa,"* or "Democracy brings you food, health, and education." This is precisely where the failure of democracy has been astonishing. The country we have today is socially more underdeveloped and economically more fragmented than in 1983.

The new protests, the lootings, the *piquetes,* and the *cacerolazos,* show the emergence of the new actors, with consequences that remain to be seen. They also represent, however, social actors that fortunately did not exist before in the massive, impressive way they shape Argentine society today, as political movements trying to express the voices of people cut off from the work force. The apex of this failure is the Alianza Government, not only because it was the last of the "normal" institutions, but because it revealed the impotence of those who, deep in their minds, also believed, with Menem, that convertibility was an "auto pilot" for the Argentine economy. They had faith that convertibility made none of their decisions risky. It only required them to follow the campaign promise of modernization without corruption, growth with convertibility.

The following exemplifies the costs of this idea. Because the monetary regime was taken as a given, the political system spent almost all of its non-renewable resources. Going back to June or July 2001:
• Menem was in jail. Although president for 10 years, democratically elected, and the man who changed the shape of the country in unexpected ways, polls showed that Menem also had the lowest support in history.
• Chacho Alvarez, who had built the political coalition to defeat and replace Menem, resigned the vice presidency, and then public life.
• De la Rúa was president of Alvarez's coalition and his popularity was in single digits, and going down.

• Finally, Domingo Cavallo, who had joined the government two months before as the last hope of once again saving the country, was already described by the media as a failure. I remember that every time he was out of the country, the media sought someone to replace him.

This leads us to the third and last point, whether convertibility, in its broader meaning of the free market reforms of the 1990s, brought a more modern society to Argentina. The four people described above are those who, from different places and toward different audiences, spent most of their political capital vehemently supporting convertibility. It is obvious that convertibility is under question. The changes, however, are again shocking, with the new private non-national sector controlling the finances of the country and the main resources of the economy. The modernization of services was so dramatic one could not recognize many parts of Buenos Aires. The redefinition of the public and private spheres of economic activity is also impressive. As expected, the private sector did make some sectors of the economy more dynamic.

The changes in the consumption boom were also impressive. For many, the dollar-based economy brought within reach imported goods and a cosmopolitan way of life. This held extraordinary political consequences for the support of these policies and tolerance of corruption and institutional deterioriation as just a "passing phenomenon." For many more, convertibility meant the possibility of thinking again toward the future and planning earnings, savings, and spending. The public sphere seemed to be creating a stable framework upon which people could develop their private lives. After decades of inflation, instability, and hyperinflation, the relative value of stability was bigger than imaginable in a normal country. The reconfiguration and modernization of the economic sphere and the perception of some people that we were becoming a normal country, however, was based on a process of double concealment: of the economic cost of that normality and the real reach of such modernization.

Once more, the Alianza played a leading role in this process. By the Alianza, I refer to a vast cultural and social movement of which De la Rúa was a minimum expression, one that included the media, intellectuals, journalists, part of the establishment within the country, part of the economic establishment out the country, and the middle class. The Alianza not only underappreciated the real macroeconomic problems of convertibility, but also overvalued its goals during the 1990s.

Since convertibility did not achieve some of the goals it proposed for a modern, globally-integrated economy, Argentina continues to be an economically closed country, according to free trade parameters, where exports represented 10-14 percent of GDP during the whole decade, even when commodity prices were very high. In comparison, the "successful" experience of the Chilean model, for example, had exports close to 30 percent. Even worse, the profile of Argentina's exports has not changed much: between seven to nine of the ten largest exports are still primary products, coming mostly from the agricultural sector. The modern sector has not absorbed the labor force eliminated from the "inefficient" and "protected" sector in all but a few years. Competition and the recession have not lowered internal prices; they actually showed little or no flexiblity at all, except in wages.

The triple crisis described, the international context, and the weakness of political power leave little room for the drastic changes that will be necessary. It is hard to forecast Duhalde's future, beyond the fact that his government is a clear product of this crisis and the complete international uncertainty about what to do with Argentina. Interestingly, the whole discussion on how to get out of the crisis looks back to 2001, as if nothing had happened at the end of the year. More recently, Argentina has been discussing ways to reduce provincial government spending, in provinces that consequently cannot expect any economic booms; and ways to concurrently increase tax collection, avoiding the potential for a recession produced by spending cuts and inflation produced by a free dollar.

It is difficult to see how these measures could work. Albert Einstein said, "Insanity is to do the same thing over and over again, expecting a different result." Similarly, the singular focus for at least the past three years on cutting the provincial deficit, should lead us to think about the problem in another way. We have to reduce the fiscal deficit – is merely to increasingly cut spending the way to do it? This strategy shows how frequently ideology, disguised as information or technical knowledge, ends up being the primary tool in understanding remote regions and problems. Prescriptions thus rely on the notion that there is one factor to change; that only through change will the country be back "on track"; that the fiscal deficit was not as part of the problem and that the cause lay instead in something previous, which once resolved, will bring health to the economy – it is amazing how we can keep pushing the wrong key.

It reminds me of a joke made famous at the end of the Soviet Union, about a worker who goes to the doctor at the Communist Party because he feels sick. He says, "Comrade doctor, I feel really ill. I drink vodka with water and I get drunk. I drink wine with water and I get drunk. I drink whisky with water and I get drunk. I don't know what to do". The doctor replies, "Comrade worker, you have to stop drinking water because it is killing you."

One of the dangers of this pessimistic landscape is that the magnitude of the crisis and the depth of the recession could be the terrain upon which to again set up policies that carry irreversible consequences. We already know that the memory of hyperinflation was the main support and strength of the economic policy developed during the 1990s. For many, some institutional, political, and economic decisions were tolerated more out of fear than conviction. It remains to be seen what the disciplinary effect will be in the coming years of this political crisis and the largest recession in Argentine history.

9

METROPOLITAN IMPACTS: FRAGMENTED SOCIETIES

BERARDO DUJOVNE

The Metropolitan Area of Buenos Aires (MABA) is comprised of the City of Buenos Aires and the twenty-four municipalities that make up Greater Buenos Aires. Containing 14 million residents, or 33.6% of Argentina's population, and with the concentration of more than half of Argentina's GDP and economic activity, the MABA is a major Latin American metropolitan region. Within the MABA, the City of Buenos Aires holds a central role: it has 3 million residents, a GDP in 2000 of approximately $80 billion, life expectancy of 72.7 years, a high level of education (one out of every five inhabitants over 24 years of age has a university degree), and an illiteracy rate of less than 1%. Additionally, with its extensive health coverage (23 doctors for every 10 thousand inhabitants) and notable cultural offerings, Buenos Aires could still be regarded as an attractive Latin American city. Yet these figures fail to reflect the reality of its surrounding metropolitan area and the impact of the recent crisis in which we are currently immersed. If asked whether Buenos Aires is an integrated and equitable urban conglomerate, whoever walks its streets would surely say no.

Looking beyond official boundaries to the entire metropolitan area and in profound contradiction to the city center, the MABA's outlying areas lack services, public spaces, and livable urban conditions. This periphery receives the greatest influx of immigrants, has high levels of pollution, and is home to the city's slums. This area, which is plagued by considerable poverty, marginality, and insecurity, however, manages to coexist alongside highly developed areas.

Urban realities can be conceived as woven from three types of fabrics: a concrete, consolidated fabric of established and developed urban conditions; a soft, undefined fabric, with few of the comforts of urbanity; and a precarious fabric, without services or paved streets, existing as an urban-peripheral zone where the city ceases to be a city. In the case of the latter, urban areas sprawl without regulations, livable conditions, or the density required to make it economically viable. There are clearly two Buenos Aires: one that is modern, able to integrate into the globalization process, and in which the best services (education, health, culture and recreation) are concentrated; and the other, which is delayed, paralyzed, forgotten. Buenos Aires today is a city without equity; segmented and dual, the lower city and the higher city are our present.

BUENOS AIRES IN HISTORICAL PERSPECTIVE

To better understand this duality, it is useful to examine the historical evolution of the city: the different shapes it has taken and the evolution of inequality in the city. The beginning of Argentina's national consolidation in 1853 and the federalization of Buenos Aires in 1880 inaugurated a period of large transformations at the turn of the 20th century. Within this agriculture-exporting country, the city was not just the space in which modernization took place but also the object of modernization. Between 1872 and 1892, Buenos Aires' notable growth transformed the "big village" into a "big city." Buenos Aires' role as a national and international center was consolidated by growth in its exports, its immigration policy, and the influx of foreign capital, which helped finance the port's construction and the development of the transport system. Buenos Aires' modernization was being carried out with the extension of train and trolley lines, the appearance of the subway in 1913, and the spread of electric service. The "1880 Generation" broke the colonial model and created the first Building Aesthetics Plan for the City of Buenos Aires. Of the many infrastructure projects included in the plan, those that were built still contribute today to distinguish their neighborhoods while those that were never carried out underscore more profoundly the unequal levels of infrastructural development among neighborhoods.

Modernization similarly affected the spread of the city's population, which grew from 187,126 inhabitants in 1869 to 1,576,814 in 1914. The downtown area grew denser and infrastructure extended to the new neighborhoods, pulling them, in turn, into the metropolitan area. Rich families left the city's southern area, which was plagued by yellow fever, and settled into large mansions in the growing and well-serviced northern area. Meanwhile, port workers and service workers crowded the tenements in the South. Buenos Aires' social geography took on a shape that persists to this day.

The city was characterized in the 1950s by urban sprawl, the product of the many factories built in Greater Buenos Aires under import-substitution policies and of the migration of Argentines attracted by the new labor market in these industrial areas. Real estate speculation thus increased and much land was left in the hands of realtors who speculated freely in the absence of state regulations. Urban sprawl expanded to productive and fertile lands that were not yet exploited, because of their low population density, and these fertile lands too fell into the hands of real estate speculators. The likelihood that this vast area would be supplied with infrastructure and services was very slight – the periphery thus expanded and the slums were born. Instead of being used for production, these vacant areas become residential zones.

Unlike the case of other Latin American metropolises, slums in Buenos Aires lie primarily in state-owned and abandoned lots. The slums are in the central area of the city and in the southern area, next to the Riachuelo. In Greater Buenos Aires, the area with the most slums is a scattered ring that coincides approximately with the first belt around the city of Buenos Aires. Slums are easily recognizable in aerial photographs, contrasting starkly with the regular, uniform lots of the rest of the city and with the nearby self-constructed neighborhoods.

In the 1960s and 1970s, the factors that had driven urban development lost their strength. Most noticeably, although urban agglomeration reached 7 million inhabitants, the metropolitan growth rate diminished as migration waned. Meanwhile, the Regulatory Office of Buenos Aires was created and developed the Guiding Plan and the Structural Outline for the Metropolitan Area, approved in 1962. The plans' aims included compensation for the unequal development of the northern and southern parts of the city, adding new green spaces and recreation areas, extending the subway system, and constructing office buildings in a strip of land parallel to the river.

The "development movement" paradigm, premised on a strong government, included all social sectors, guaranteeing the necessary conditions of social mobility and equal access to opportunity. It faced, however, two Buenos Aires: the formal city with a high quality of life, which was consolidated and sprawled over a standardized grid; and the informal city, lacking services and encompassing a region without such an ordered pattern. Only at the end of the 1970s did the province of Buenos Aires pass a law (Law 8912) to regulate urban growth and ban the creation of new urbanized areas without also providing sanitation services. Unfortunately, the law was approved only when the most significant urban growth had already been consolidated without this necessary infrastructure.

As in other parts of the world at the end of the 1980s and during the 1990s, the government was withdrawing, not only from its subsidiary activities but also from its most basic functions. Vigorous sales and land concessions marked the city, at a cost to public space. Within such a framework, the upper-middle class sought shelter in gated neighborhoods with private security in the enclaves of the northern suburbs. The construction of highways facilitated this movement, to the detriment of public works that improved and extended the public transport networks. These factors triggered processes of urban deterioration that are hard to reverse in many downtown neighborhoods, and that worsened with the exodus of many services and administrative companies to the suburban areas.

Thus, over the decades, there was a growing process of social fragmentation with a clear physical backdrop. In the following pages, the current situation will be briefly described, and some suggestions for the Metropolitan Area will be presented.

INEQUITY AND LIVING CONDITIONS

It is imperative to note that the process of social fragmentation has accelerated in recent years, with an intense concentration of income that did not, as many had predicted, extend to the rest of society. The exclusion of millions of Argentines is unprecedented in its history, with spatial-physical consequence of slum overpopulation in the environmentally vital areas of the MABA. Conversely, high-income enclaves emerged along the northern corridor, more than 40 kilometers from the city's downtown. Surrounded by areas of extreme scarcity and poverty, these enclaves exhibit a carefully designed inner space and are closed to the outer world, penetrable only with private access.

In addition to these starkly contrasting inequalities, the government failed to adequately address the quality of living conditions. Its actions presumed that the housing problem could be tackled by simply building houses. The number of houses built was a simple estimation, quantitative and homogeneous, based on figures of the unmet housing needs of those who could not afford them. It did not include an examination on the "living conditions deficit," crowded houses, lack of infrastructure and services, inaccessibility, etc. Reality has demonstrated the limits and inefficiency of these policies, which made few improvements in the population's quality of life because they did not grapple with the complexity and diversity of the problem.

In the city of Buenos Aires, data from the 1991 census shows that the quality of housing of 4.3 percent of total households is inadequate in some way. This fact, however, masks the larger region's great asymmetries. In contrast, in the 22 municipalities of the MABA, over 25 percent of households are inadequate. Of the over 3 million households registered in the MABA, nearly 600,000, or 20 percent of the total, are inadequate. Surely, given the observable inequality among neighborhoods of Greater Buenos Aires, even greater asymmetries would surface along the north-south division.

ACCESSIBILITY AND TRANSPORTATION

In recent years, the transportation system of the MABA has been greatly transformed because of two principal factors: the impact on the transportation system of privatization, deregulation, and government concessions for railway infrastructure; and new patterns of land use. Consequently, this new framework has shifted demand among the different means of transportation. The number of private automobiles has risen and railway services have improved. In turn, fewer people turn to buses; in recent months, there has been a decline in bus use throughout the entire system.

Since a variety of organizations control the national, municipal, and provincial transportation companies in the MABA, the transportation system often lacks coordination and operates along several levels of conflict. Although the local government hears grievances against the system, it is unable to effectively intervene to improve it.

INFRASTRUCTURE AND THE ENVIRONMENT

In various municipalities of the MABA, the infrastructure is notably limited, in some cases reaching less than 10 percent of the population. With such poor infrastructure, these areas benefit from few health, education, or economic development services. Additionally, they reveal the magnitude of inequality when compared to the almost 100 percent infrastructure coverage in the city of Buenos Aires. In Buenos Aires, 99 percent of the population has sewage systems compared to 45 percent in the 24 municipalities of the MABA. Although the municipalities fare better in accessibility to potable water, inequality between Buenos Aires and the other areas within the greater MABA persists: 99% percent of Buenos Aires has potable water, yet in the 24 municipalities, only 73% is covered. Potable water and sewage services are being expanded in marginal zones and low-income neighborhoods. However, while the population of the city of Buenos Aires has remained steady for the last fifty years, the areas in which services are scarcest or inexistent are precisely those where population growth has been greatest, further straining services in those areas.

PROPOSALS

The socio-territorial conditions described thus far have a historical legacy and have been further worsened by the recent crisis. With an aim to finding a solution to the current situation, the following proposals include institutional, physical, emergency policy, and strategic development policy dimensions. These proposals are designed to address the current emergency, but carry relevance for the future at large, constituting ways to definitively rectify the MABA's conditions of inequality. Towards that goal, the School of Architecture, Design, and Planning of the

University of Buenos Aires is committed to shaping itself into a think tank of ideas and proposals to provide relief in the national crisis. We have invited students, research centers, and institutions to search with us for alternative solutions.

Institutional Proposals

In considering action plans for the MABA, it must be remembered that it is not only a territorially large region, but one of great institutional complexity as well. The MABA is comprised of one autonomous city and 24 municipalities that answer both to their respective local governments and to that of the province of Buenos Aires. Furthermore, the national government controls some aspects of the MABA's organization and service provisioning. A complex of influences affects each jurisdiction.

The principal challenge for management strategies, therefore, is to identify coordinated projects that entities with diverse jurisdictional influences can carry out. They would then be able to act on issues that go beyond their own administrative districts. Such a situation demands institutionally articulated programs since there currently is no coordination between the city and the municipalities or even among the municipalities themselves. The following are proposals for institutional management that should be implemented:

• Integrate the municipalities, to strengthen the public perspective;
• Organize the management process: this will depend on the degree of integration to face sectoral or territorial problems. Municipalities may not all be included.

• Strengthen local management, which grants policing power and control over metropolitan issues to local entities;
• Promote efficient and rational use of resources, with the goal of guaranteeing equitable socio-physical development. All actors must be included when allocating resources and establishing priorities and control.

Physical Proposals

In terms of the physical territory of the MABA, I will cite some proposals from the Urban Environment Plan of the city of Buenos Aires – a similar plan, unfortunately, does not exist for the MABA. The plan outlined five factors that would produce improved quality of life for the population: competition, equality, sustainability, good governance, and stability.

Those proposals that tend to coincide with increased opportunities for the inhabitants are particularly important, since spatial-physical conditions that are more equitable would undoubtedly improve living conditions. The glaring inequality between the northern and southern areas of the city is clear; for example, the large differences in child mortality rates between the two areas results from the southern population's lack of medical insurance and the structural poverty that governs their lives. To confront the problems of the South, the Urban Environment Plan suggests programmatic intervention for the renewal, improved accessibility of, and integration of these sectors with the rest of the MABA and the city. For example, the "Green Corridor from the West" project seeks to eliminate the physical barrier that separates the North from the South, and the "Green Corridor from the South" project aims to revitalize the southern zone through parks and green areas along current and future avenues.

Emergency policies

At the School for Architecture, Design, and Planning, we have initially employed two distinct approaches: looking at theory and aiming for direct action.

Theory, embodied in reflection and analysis, guides policy to respond to the needs of vulnerable areas and slums within the MABA. To improve the lives of the urban population to adequacy, policy strategy must recover and renovate the most deteriorated and precarious areas. Improvements should not only take form physically in housing, but should also occur in public spaces and services. In understanding and transforming the city, we at the School have drawn from those aspects of urban development policy that give priority to the reintegration of historically-neglected areas, such as tenements and slums. These marginal areas have potential for recovery, and are capable of renovation, improvement, and integration at the neighborhood level. The local level can prompt change, with the active participation of neighborhood residents and through the rational and articulated deployment of already existing private and public resources; the incentive for growth and integration in this process must build up from what is already in place.

The household is only one aspect of the problem – the axis of the solutions involves several factors. Urban services must expand to cover neglected areas. Construction of a suitable transportation system can connect and extend the urban infrastructure. The urban system must break the pattern of isolation and instead look towards integration. Recovery, therefore, will be the fruit of an urban system that builds better transportation, infrastructure, and livelihoods. Furthermore, recovery will be best achieved if area residents actively carry out the proposal.

In terms of direct action, we have begun a series of actions, including:

• Transforming abandoned factories into permanent residences for the newly poor;

• Fostering micro-enterprises aligned with the most vulnerable social sectors and the unemployed;

• Creating a machinery bank for research equipment and technical training, to promote creative solutions to unmet basic necessities. Several such solutions include reusing plastic bottles abandoned in garbage bags as construction materials, forming clay into ecological bricks, and paving streets with recycled plastic blocks in Villa Gesell. We hope to replicate and further build upon these experimental projects.

• Designing a series of handbooks, with the Municipal Housing Commission of the City of Buenos Aires, that give technical support to the self-led construction projects within the city's slums.

The School continues to develop other initiatives that apply scientific and technical possibilities to bring the most vulnerable, and often excluded, sectors back into society. These proposals do not in themselves constitute a base on which to build a modern Argentina. Yet given the gravity of the current social tension, implementing such relief policies and opening the possibility of social advancement toward a better future is vital.

Strategic Development Planning at the National Level

Finally, a plan for strategic development at the national level, one in which the MABA holds a role, needs to be developed. This discussion must include examination of which economic bases of growth would achieve a more equitable internal redistribution. It is necessary to rethink the types of productive activities and areas of science and technology to promote; a process for including all social sectors in these proposals; and the socio-physical adaptations to be promoted by the MABA towards a future Strategic Plan for National Development. Such reassessments should take full advantage of the multitude of university graduates and the variety of knowledge they can offer Argentina.

The only alternative that remains for our society to emerge from this crisis and recover towards development will be found in strategic thinking, working from the themes outlined in this article. Such strategic thinking would produce active social policies that can help relieve the delicate and immediate social situation. Only in this way will we be able to move beyond the inequality that has become entrenched in our society.

The challenge to be confronted is a significant one. In contemplating the mechanisms that will make a solution possible, it is only with a comprehensive vision that we can take maximum advantage of resources to produce true modernization in the country.

IV

INTERNATIONAL AND
REGIONAL DIMENSIONS

10
INTERNATIONAL, REGIONAL AND NATIONAL RESPONSIBILITIES

JOSEPH S. TULCHIN

Examining the Argentine crisis in terms of "responsibility" conveys the implication made by many economists and representatives of multinational economic and financial institutions – principally the IMF and the U.S., and in particular U.S. Treasury Secretary Paul O'Neill. That is, "How can a sovereign nation deal with its responsibilities after errors and default on its financial obligations?" The burden of the task is thus framed in economic terms and focuses on Argentina's plans to pull itself out of the crisis. Such an approach belies the full scope of the issue. Just as the fiscal crisis must be understood in its political, social, and cultural dimensions, policy solutions must consider political and strategic contexts, extending beyond economics to foreign policy. Working with the IMF, to take one example, is more than a dialogue between economists and technocrats, it is high politics and diplomacy. Foreign policy is thus a question of the available opportunities, rather than a matter of responsibility. Given the cri-

sis in which it is now enmeshed, what are the foreign policy opportunities available for Argentina to poise itself to
emerge from the crisis?

As the current Duhalde government and its predeces-
sors, De La Rúa in particular, adopted Carlos Menem's
foreign policy with the most insignificant of changes, it is
worthwhile to examine Menem's foreign policy approach
to understand the current context. Starting from a populist
electoral campaign, Peronist President Menem surprisingly turned to a neoliberal, open-market orientation, with
Domingo Cavallo as economy minister and a succession
of ministers with equally orthodox macroeconomic policies. Menem also cast aside the myth that Argentina would
soon become one of the world's great powers, if not the
greatest, seeking instead to forge alliances to become, as
he often put it, *del premier mundo*, of the first world, and
a "normal country." In the 50 years before Menem, the
myth of greatness brought frequently adversarial relations
with the United States and the larger community of developed countries, including Europe. Menem instead
reached out to the United States to provide necessary
inputs and bolster Argentina's image as a "reliable partner." As such, Argentina could attract foreign capital to
modernize the economy and, by privatizing old government-run corporations, transform them into conduits for
cutting edge technology.

Privatization was thus not only intended to generate
profits, but to enable companies to provide a level of services *del premier mundo* to consumers. The Argentine tele-
phone company before privatization is remembered less
for its unprofitability than for its inability to deliver tele-
phones and services to consumers. Similarly, the national
petroleum company was criticized less for its unprofitability or for the 50,000 members of the bureaucracy on its
payrolls who did no work, than for its failure to produce

the petroleum and natural resources required by the country's economy. Today, both are capable of fulfilling these basic functions, with some limitations, as are other privatized companies.

More importantly, Menem aimed to reinsert Argentina into the world system as a major player, or at least one that would assume increasing importance. Due to the excesses of the military dictatorship, Argentina had been excluded from virtually all international geopolitical activities. As reasonable as this objective appears, there is also an enduring element of Argentine exceptionalism, as Menem's cabinet has noted, in its presumed ability to return to its path of preordained greatness by overcoming its pariah status. Menem's foreign policy retained a notion of Argentina's greatness, a notion that he had identified as a hindrance to relations with the developed world.

Today there appears a generational gap in the perception of Argentina's greatness and its place in world affairs. Numerous public opinion polls show that generally, those under 35 years of age overwhelmingly accept the notion of Argentina as a modest country. Having spent most of their adult lives in the 1990s, they enjoyed a stability that was especially pronounced as access to the world outside Argentina provided a global context to their lives. In contrast, older Argentines remain more reluctant to let go of the notion that their country can overtake the United States as a world power in the foreseeable future, and thus hold such complacency with being a middle-class country with some disdain.

Menem's foreign policy was also constrained by its lack of flexibility. Unlike comparable countries in weak geopolitical positions, Argentina had no sense of multiple objectives or strategies, focusing instead on pleasing the United States. Inflexibility is manifest in the De La Rúa government's political reaction to convertibility, which had been under public debate a year and a half before the crisis. However logical Roberto Rocca's proposal for its elimination in 1999, it was restrained by a fear of taking foreign or economic policy action that could threaten the gains of the last decade or Argentina's image as a "reliable partner."

Given a foreign policy approach with a legacy of inflexibility and statism, but general success, a number of opportunities remain for the Duhalde government. These opportunities have not been threatened or diminished by the crisis. First, Argentina has the opportunity to engage in international anti-terrorism efforts. The United States, United Nations, Israel, and a number of organizations have approached Argentina to cooperate on the Triple Frontier, the tri-border area between Argentina, Paraguay, and Brazil. The area, particularly the Paraguayan town Ciudad del Este, has been a haven for terrorists and is believed to have been the base for the bombings in Buenos Aires of the Israeli Embassy in 1992 and an Argentine Jewish community center in 1994.

Despite international pressure to address these terrorist activities, the Menem government took very little action. De La Rúa's efforts were greater, but constrained by emerging frictions between the restructured Argentine intelligence agencies and local CIA and FBI agents. President Duhalde has a renewed opportunity to collaborate with the United States and Paraguay, which is now actively pursuing this terrorist cell and may convince Brazil to join efforts. Intelligence sharing with the United States, Western Europe, and Interpol would be a valued contribution that costs nothing and is easily accomplished. In a similar fashion, Argentina can collaborate and contribute to efforts to combat money laundering.

Two other areas that Menem undertook to a limited extent but can be more actively pursued by Duhalde are peacekeeping and arms control. Even in the context of the current crisis, participation in these efforts is possible. Argentina would gain a high profile with little cost. These possible areas of action share another feature extremely important for framing Argentina's post-default foreign policy and position in world affairs: they involve multilateral cooperation and working with international organizations.

On the economic front, trade strategy and policy is a foreign policy opportunity crucial to reactivating Argentina's economy. Indeed, the foreign ministry is currently formulating a clear, export-oriented trade strategy. Devaluation will help primary product exporters and those who can quickly adapt to the artificial currency barrier protections. Small manufacturing will have an immediate advantage while creating many jobs relative to the amount invested.

Furthermore, a trade strategy that is successful in the short- and medium term must incorporate multilateral organizations. Argentina should enthusiastically participate in and support the rules of the Cairns Group and the WTO, even when some in Europe block crucial Argentine products. Flexibility will prove ever more important as some Argentine products will enjoy U.S. support while others will run against U.S. interests. Trade strategy will reinforce the need for multinational collaboration, already fundamental to areas such as peacekeeping and arms control explored earlier.

More strategically, Argentina must again be flexible and mediate its relationships with MERCOSUR and the United States. Looking to MERCOSUR would mean sidling up to Brazil, but relations with the United States would be under conditions of default to an administration that may not be interested in providing such a level of support. As such, if an examination of the U.S.-Argentine relationship over the next one to three years suggests that it would no longer provide the benefits envisioned by Menem, an alternative mode of insertion into the international arena is indispensable.

The one difficult but critical element for pursuing the foreign policy approach described above is government capability. The De La Rúa government, however, frequently demonstrated government incapacity, evidenced in part by the federalist split. As with fiscal policy, successful foreign policy requires legitimacy. The current government appears to understand this requirement, as it has repeatedly told the IMF that it could not meet certain demands, not for technical reasons but because they cannot do certain things without, in the words of a cabinet member, "being lynched." This illustrates Duhalde's prudence in dealing with the IMF and other external actors, to cover his domestic front as he negotiates internationally. While his financial team deliberates the point at which the political benefit of allowing themselves to be pushed by the IMF is trumped by defying it, at the moment, an agreement with the IMF is of primary importance.

Finally, the reaction of the other South American countries to Argentina's crisis is extremely important to the immediate future of Argentine foreign policy. While some leaders have been enormously supportive, it remains unclear how this will translate into specific actions. Greater help and support from the region would do much to enable Argentina to cleanse itself of its sin of default.

V

Lessons for Development

11

THE LESSONS OF ARGENTINA
FOR DEVELOPMENT
IN LATIN AMERICA

JOSEPH STIGLITZ

Several questions are repeatedly being asked throughout Latin America: Why has globalization reform failed us? Where do go from here? Those two questions are, in fact, very closely related, because one of the main items in the economic reform agenda was that globalization had enormous promise for the countries of Latin America. A related question is why is there such hypocrisy in the North, and what should Latin Americans do about it?

In terms of the first question, why has globalization reform failed us? There is very little doubt that if you were to visit Latin America from another planet and looked at the data over the last 40 or 50 years, you would not approach this last decade with a great deal of euphoria. Latin America has gone through a number of different stages. There was a stage of import substitution in the 1950s, 1960s, and 1970s. At the end of that stage, there was an enormous amount of debt borrowing – or "recycling petrodollars" – that was followed by a debt crisis.

One interpretation of the debt crisis was that low interest rates induced countries to borrow. Real interest rates were, in fact, negative during the period, so that borrowing and taking on increasing debt was prudent.

Later, for reasons having nothing to do with Latin America, but in response to inflation and anti-inflationary sentiment in the United States, the U.S. Federal Reserve raised interest rates to very high levels. The high rates were beyond the ability of Latin America to bear, leading to the debt crisis of the 1980s. It took a decade for that debt crisis to be adequately resolved. Wide reforms followed at the end of the 1980s and the beginning of the 1990s, and were considered the new democratic reform agenda. By 2002, we have now experienced a decade of economic growth under reform.

One of the interpretations of the failure of the earlier import substitution strategy was that it ended with the debt crisis imposed from the outside because of high interest rates. The high interest rates were unexpected and higher than had ever been seen before. Although general theories of efficient risk bearing place the burden on rich countries, the debtor countries were made to bear the risk instead and the Latin American countries were not able to do so.

The other interpretation is that, in fact, the import substitution strategy was itself doomed and that the debt crisis just brought it to its end. The countries had learned the lessons of the failures of the import substitution strategy and they went to the alternative – a strategy of reform that has helped to account for a decade of success.

However, data on economic growth in the 1990's shows that after a few good years in the beginning, overall growth for the decade is a little higher than half what it was in the 60's and 70's; thus, it is not correct to describe the reform decade of the 1990s as a successful decade.

Economic growth in the 90s was roughly half of what it was during the 50s, 60s, and 70s, which was a long period of sustained growth.

The reform decade of the 1990s is even worse, because the growth that has occurred has been shared very inequitably. One of the countries that has been a relative success story is Mexico. However, almost all of Mexico's growth, as the Inter-American Development Bank has pointed out, occurred in the upper 30 percent of the population, and most of the growth occurred in the upper 10 percent. People at the bottom were actually worse off.

Therefore, both in terms of growth and in terms of equity, the so-called reform decade has hardly been one that one can call a resounding success. To make matters worse, the star pupil, Argentina, has now gone into what might be described as a meltdown. There are many interpretations of what went wrong with the star pupil. Until Argentina lost its star status, its performance was constantly praised. One of the reasons Argentina's debt grew so much was that the IMF and international bankers said that the country was a good place to land. They lent money at attractive terms and Argentina borrowed. Even at the end, however, Argentina's debt-GDP ratio was only around 45 percent. In contrast, Japan's debt-GDP ratio is around 130 percent; Belgium's is over 100 percent. Argentina was not the most profligate country in the world, which is the impression one would have if one listened to the IMF rhetoric.

In fact, from the budgetary point of view, Argentina had a primary surplus in the 1990s. The term primary surplus refers to the difference between its revenues and its expenditures, excluding interest payments – if interest payments are excluded, Argentina was in surplus. Argentina's net deficit would also have not been very large, except for reasons beyond its control: the world had a global financial crisis in 1997-98. Argentina cannot be blamed for the global financial crisis, which began in Thailand and Indonesia and spread to Korea, Russia, and Brazil.

One can blame the IMF for the way the global financial crisis was mismanaged. Their mismanagement, at the global level and in the Asian financial crisis, led to very high interest rates, particularly after the problems in Russia. Even though Argentina's debt-GDP ratio was very moderate and, in fact, in many senses low, the interest rates it faced became very high. There is a paradox: if creditors believe that a country is going into default, they will charge very high interest rates. Furthermore, if they charge very high interest rates, countries will go into default. There are theoretical models showing that there are a multiplicity of equilibriums in which – with enough pessimism – countries can arrive at a self-fulfilling prophecy of a default.

In a way, the IMF served as a partial ringleader for the default, because it helped convince the creditors that Argentina had fundamental problems. Rather than saying, "Argentina has only a 45 percent debt-GDP ratio," the IMF said, "This country does not know how to manage itself." It did in Argentina just as it did in many of the countries in East Asia, where the IMF advertised incompetence. One cannot say that there was no corruption or that everything was run perfectly, but there are no governments, including the United States, where things are run perfectly. By instead advertising all these problems, it helped moved the economy to what might be called "a bad equilibrium," in which everybody believed in the default that led to the high interest rates that led, in turn, to default.

The lessons of Argentina's failed policy can be generalized. One concerns the fixed exchange rate system. In 1989, Argentina had a problem of high inflation and, in that context, adopting a fixed exchange rate – sometimes called the nominal anchor – was thought to be a way of bringing down the inflation. It worked, but inflation is not an end in itself. People do not live off inflation numbers – they live off growth and food, but not inflation numbers.

The single-minded focus on inflation led to some very adverse consequences. It was thought that since inflation was down, the country's performance was a success and its problems were solved. That assessment, of course, was wrong. The economy did start to grow, but one has to look at this growth in perspective. Whenever an economy goes through a period of zero growth, very low growth, or negative growth, there is normally a catch-up period. So during this catch-up period, it is difficult to interpret growth: Is the perceived growth the robust growth that follows a period of stagnation, because good policies are really the beginning of a new era? Or is the growth the catch-up from the past era, and one that, once the economy has caught up, will go into a more normal phase?

The evidence in Latin America is that growth in the early period, 1990-94, was a catch-up, not part of a sustained higher level of economic growth. It certainly was not sustained and some people would say it was not sustainable. Economic growth only lasted through 1994, when the *tequila* crisis hit. It was interesting to see the lesson that was drawn from the *tequila* crisis. Upon seeing how badly Argentina was battered, with soaring unemployment and a weakened economy, one could gather that the fixed exchange rate system really had some problems. When crises occur, such as the Mexican crisis in which exchange rates changed very dramatically, a fixed exchange rate becomes misaligned relative to other exchange rates.

That, however, was not the lesson most others drew. They said, if Argentina managed to survive the crisis of

1994-95, it could survive any other crisis, so the existing system of fixed exchange rates should be maintained. Then, of course, the world went through the period of the East Asia crisis, where exchange rates in many of the other developing countries came down markedly. This was followed by a period in which the dollar became still more overvalued. It should be remembered that when the peso was tied with the dollar, an overvalued dollar meant that the peso was doubly overvalued. Finally, when Brazil crashed and its exchange rate went down and continued to go down, Argentina's exchange rate relative to its trading partners in MERCOSUR became more and more misaligned.

Argentina's "hitching its stars" to the U.S. dollar was just a very foolish policy. It was obviously foolish in the beginning: it could have been justified as a way to stop inflation. But as soon as inflation was stopped, it seems quite obvious that Argentina should have moved away from that exchange rate policy. Nevertheless, the IMF fixated on controlling inflation and thus encouraged Argentina to retain the peg with the dollar.

One quite interesting aspect of this situation in terms of its political economy is that the IMF and others who came to Argentina were very successful in convincing the Argentine people on this policy; in 1999-2001, popular support for maintaining the peg to the dollar was very strong. That sentiment tied the government's hands in a way. At the time, polls reported that 50-70 percent of the people wanted to maintain the peg with the dollar. That meant that the scope for discretion of the government might have been reduced. It would have taken a strong action and a strong degree of persuasion to change the policy.

I had conversations with people who said that if we lost the peg with the dollar, Argentina would go back to the hyperinflation of the 1980s. When they were reminded that Brazil went off its peg and avoided inflation, they would reply that Brazil is Brazil, and we are Argentina. That is a very hard argument to contend with – they are Argentina, and Brazil is Brazil – but unfortunately, that was the end of the conversation. It is, however, an important part of the political backdrop, because it did constrain the government. And it is one of the examples where if you engage in "education or mis-education" of the populace in a particular set of doctrines, you can reduce their degrees of freedom, making it very difficult for them to get out of the problems they face.

The fixed exchange rate was clearly one of the major problems Argentina faced, making it very difficult to resume economic growth. But it was only one; another was the fact that most of its banks had been sold to foreign banks. Again, the IMF and many of the outsiders were very proud of this, saying that with foreign banks, Argentina would have a very solid banking system. They forgot a couple of things. First, with capital market liberalization, people can still take their money out of banks. Secondly, even with good management, if everybody takes their money out of a bank, the bank has problems.

The banking system thus wound up having a great deal of problems. There is another point that is even more fundamental. Requiring banks to hold only U.S. Treasury bills could produce a sound banking system. The problem, however, is that the bank is not performing the functions it should, such as promoting economic growth, except in the United States.

The idea of a bank is that it is supposed to lend money to promote economic growth. There is a proclivity for foreign banks to lend to IBMs and Coca-Colas and things that may be good for the economy, but do not promote domestic growth, such as small- and medium-size enterprises do. The lack of credit for firms was one of the problems that Argentine businesses were increasingly facing. The government did set up a ministry to try to address the problem – recognizing that the lack of capital flow to small- and medium-sized enterprises was stifling growth – but it did not handle the problem adequately. The privatization of the financial sector proved to be part of the Argentine problem because of a lack of the capital necessary for sustained economic growth.

There were also aspects of the privatization program that were problematic. Privatization occurred without the establishment of an effective competitive structure. Even worse, it indexed the price of some utilities to the U.S. dollar. This was particularly problematic, because the theory of adjustment of the IMF and others who advocated the fixed exchange rate system, held that without exchange rate adjustment, it is necessary to adjust domestic prices. While domestic prices were adjusted, this adjustment was not sufficiently large at a time when wages were falling at 30 percent per year.

Therefore, wages and prices were falling but utility rates were fixed in terms of U.S. dollars. The utilities received more and more money and weakened the overall economy. This should not have come as a surprise, since the theory of exchange rate adjustment held that there should be accompanying declines in prices and wages. To maintain this theory of adjustment while indexing the prices charged by private utilities was really malfeasance.

The final blow to Argentina, as the economy began to have these problems and interest rates rose from lack of confidence, was the official response of cutting expenditures. Cutting expenditures had the effect of reducing aggregate demand; reducing aggregate lowered GDP; and lowering GDP lowered tax revenues. The goal behind this chain was to bring the government into fiscal balance. Of course, it failed, and predictably so.

The irony of this situation, of course, is that these policies had been discussed at length in long-standing debates. During the Great Depression, people like Andrew Mellon argued that the United States should break out of the depression by restoring its fiscal balance through raising taxes and cutting expenditures. At the same time, Keynes proposed an alternative approach to macroeconomics by stimulating the economy. Ironically, this is the same Keynes who had an important role in establishing the IMF, which was founded on the idea that, in the event of the kind of crisis that Argentina faced, it would lend money to help it finance deficits. There were to be conditions, stipulating that countries pursue expansionary fiscal policies.

It is interesting to note that the first example of IMF conditionality was in the late 1940s in Belgium, whose policy was excessively contractionary. Yet, sometime between the end of the 1940s and now, the IMF got mixed up. Just as my students always tell me I make sign mistakes when I am doing math on the board, I think the IMF has made a sign mistake. They thought expansionary meant contractionary and went around telling everybody to have contractionary policies, although I think there is a deeper explanation than that.

In my judgment, it is unambiguously the case that the failure in Argentina can be attributed to a whole series of mistakes from exchange rate policy, to fiscal policy, to privatization policies, and culminating in the disaster that began in December; a disaster that is, unfortunately, continuing. The IMF is continuing to recommend that the country persist with a contractionary fiscal policy, which will force the economy deeper into recession.

I had worried for a long time that these policies were not sustainable. Argentina has had double-digit unemployment rates since the *tequila* crisis. And in the end, for many who had been watching Argentina closely, the surprise was not that riots broke out in December 2001, but that it took so long for them do to so. What is commendable is the patience of the Argentine people. It was not that they eventually gave up in disillusionment at a set of policies that had failed – and for which there was no prospect of any alternative. The problem is that the current government is offering, in many ways, a continuation of the same contractionary policies.

I will later put all of this into perspective, but I want to put the Argentine experience into a little bit broader framework. As I said, the second question that I hear repeatedly as I travel around Latin America concerns the hypocrisy, the double standard between the north and the south, and what can be done about it.

The example of macroeconomic policy is perhaps the most dramatic, and one about which I have been asked most frequently this fall. Although pulling out of it now, the United States has been in recession probably since March 2001 – and during that recession, everybody agreed, including both political parties – that there ought to be a stimulatory and expansionary fiscal policy. Regardless of whether the policy the Republicans crafted was in fact expansionary rather than redistributive, it was advertised as an expansionary policy in the rhetoric, at least. Nobody said that the United States should contract. Similarly, Japan has been having an economic downturn. For the last six to seven years, U.S. administrations, both parties, and Presidents Clinton and Bush, have repeatedly given very severe lectures to Japan that it should have expansionary fiscal policy. The poor Japanese know it by heart now; they can play it back for you.

Expansion has been the standard line. Yet, when I am in Latin America, I am repeatedly asked, we do not understand, there seem to be two economic laws; how could that be? When a recession occurs in Latin America, contractionary fiscal policies are pushed. The real problem, of course, is that many Latin American students went to the same graduate courses and actually read good textbooks that discuss expansionary fiscal policy. None of the textbooks that I know of actually recommends contractionary fiscal policies in a recession. Latin Americans have read these textbooks and say, we do not understand, the IMF seems to be using a different textbook from the rest of the world. Unfortunately, I can not give them a good response.

That is not the only example of this hypocrisy. President Cardoso of Brazil recently gave a very scathing speech, pointing out that the IMF uses a double standard in its accounting systems — on whether the deficits of state corporations are included in the overall balance sheet of the government. There is in fact a whole set of peculiar accounting issues that have plagued Latin America.

As a result of these accounting issues, Latin American countries are told they have deficits. Using good accounting procedures, however, the accounts would look very different. It is almost as if there was a deliberate decision to use account procedures to make Latin America look worse, compared to the accounting procedures used in Europe. President Cardoso asked why such a double standard exists; I am asked the same question in Mexico and other countries — and again, there is no adequate answer. Occasionally, the IMF will say that it will look into the issue; but this is not a new issue — it has been going on for a long time.

Of course, the most grating issue has to do with trade; the developing countries have been repeatedly told that they ought to liberalize and take down their trade barriers. Yet, the U.S. just imposed tariffs on steel and is now engaged in increasing its agricultural subsidies beyond all prior levels. For the developing countries, of course, agricultural exports are absolutely vital. If Argentina had good access to international markets, it could alleviate many of its problems.

There is therefore a great deal of dissatisfaction with the economic policies and the rules of the game imposed by the international community. That raises two questions: Where to go from here?, which I will answer in two parts; and, What should Argentina – and in a broader sense, other Latin American countries – do?

In terms of Argentina – we should admit that we do not really know what will work. We do have fair confidence, however, about what will not work; mainly, that continuing contractionary fiscal policies will make the economy plummet. There is a responsibility of the international community to help Argentina. Largely, Argentina's predicament – while its government certainly has had some role – is tied to the international community, particularly to the advice the international community gave to the Argentine government and the willingness with which it lent money when things were good. Changing circumstances led to much higher interest rates and the international community has some responsibility.

The most important point is not to bail out banks – that is not really the priority; the real priority is job creation in one form or another. How does an economy start growing again? In terms of job creation, it is by really opening markets to the goods that are produced in these countries.

An important initiative would be for Europe and the United States to recognize that Argentina is in an emergency. In a way, the WTO recognizes the need for special actions in the event of an emergency and allows countries special protective measures. The safeguard measures are a partial example of that. One ought to consider an alternative perspective: looking not at the protective measures to be taken by Argentina – because those will not help Argentina very much – but rather, what the international community can do by opening up its markets, as an emergency measure to help countries that are in desperate straits?

This would mean, for example, a temporary suspension of Most Favored Nation provisions for say, a period of a year or two during which the United States would open its markets to Argentine goods without duty until Argentina can restore growth. This measure would have a miniscule effect on the rest of the world; it would have an enormous effect on Argentina. So I think this is where the international community ought to begin. I am actually not optimistic about this happening, although I am not completely pessimistic. I have talked to people in Europe about this idea, and it has some resonance there.

Since this may or may not happen, it is important for Argentina to look next door to its neighbor in Brazil and to use this as an occasion to perhaps strengthen MERCOSUR. It should perhaps go beyond the trade agreement that constituted MERCOSUR and consider a currency union with Brazil. What Argentina will need at some point is a restoration of confidence in its currency. Some people are talking about dollarization. I want to be provocative: I think returning to dollarization would be a mistake, even links to the dollar at the value level. There are better prospects of linking it to its next-door neighbor.

Finally, a point that I made before – the fact that it has a primary surplus means that its revenues exceed its expenditures if you exclude interest payments. Thus, if Argentina suspends interest payments, it has room for increasing expenditures that would increase aggregate demand and therefore stimulate its economy. I do not want to underestimate the consequences of those kinds of suspensions for the disruption of the financial system and in turn, the consequences of the disruption of the financial system for the overall functioning of the economy. Such measures cannot be taken lightly, but given the current circumstances, the alternatives that the current government is pursuing do not look likely to get it out of its predicaments.

Finally, let me say just a few words about the broader issues of Latin America – much of which also applies to other countries in the developing world. In Latin America, and Argentina in particular, capital market liberalization with more broad openness presents enormous risks to countries and makes life difficult, to put it mildly. It makes economic management very difficult. Some countries have learned how to manage in that very difficult situation. Chile has done that by restricting and intervening in, for at least long periods, the free flow of capital. Other countries are finding clever ways of intervening in the free flow of capital without opprobrium of the IMF. They have done it more subtly through the banking system, rather than calling it capital market regulations or controls as those are words you are not supposed to use. More clever ways of stabilizing capital flows must be found. A number of countries today are engaged in doing that, but one has to begin with the recognition that open capital market macroeconomics is fundamentally different from the kind of macroeconomics that once prevailed. It has a lot more instability.

The second observation I think that one has to recognize is that a lot of the political economy and rhetoric associated with fixed exchange rates is wrong and misguided. The rhetoric was that the fixed exchange rate would provide discipline, and that discipline would lead to strong economic growth. The same kind of vocabulary is used for capital market globalization, that opening capital markets brings the corresponding discipline, which is good for economic growth. Everybody believes in this concept of discipline. Actually, these are very anti-democratic concepts, because they are saying they do not really believe in democratic processes as discipline devices. Looking at it another way, if you are going to have a disciplinarian, choose one that is not too erratic. The nature of the capital market as a disciplinarian is very erratic, punishing even when the country is not naughty. That is one of the things that happened to Argentina – a good disciplinarian punishes only when naughty, and for the right things.

The other problem is that short-term capital markets discipline countries in terms of that about which markets care. These concerns can be markedly different from those of long-term investment or labor. The contrast that I sometimes imagine would be a world in which we have free mobility of labor, rather than free mobility of capital. Imagine what would happen with free mobility of labor if a country started having bad pollution policies, causing people to have trouble breathing. All of a sudden, everybody would disappear from the country, and all that would remain would be machines. Well, that would be a very different kind of discipline, and policy would then run in a very different way. Capital market liberalization does lead to a discipline but the question is, is it the right discipline? It is an erratic discipline, and it is not even clear it is a discipline related to economic growth – the statistics show that it is not.

The other aspect is if a disciplinarian is too tough, discipline does not work. That is basically what happened to Argentina. The IMF said Argentina had to have flexible wages, meaning that the country had to be able to cut wages 20 or 30 percent a year or some such large number. The government also had to be able to cut budgets more than any government normally is able to cut. Yes, it is possible to imagine a world in which wages easily fell by

20 to 30 percent and governments easily cut budgets overnight by 20 percent or 30 percent, but I have not seen any governments like that. One could imagine such a government in a thought experiment. Without such a government and with the added stipulation that a degree of flexibility is required, which is never achieved, then the imposed system is an invitation for disaster. That is essentially what the IMF did. So, the second broad point is to think very carefully about the word discipline and what disciplines are imposed.

The third point is that countries should be very skeptical about borrowing abroad, or borrowing in general. Argentina did not borrow very much and it got into a very serious problem, from which I think any calculus of the benefits received in extra growth in, say, 1996 or 1997 is far, far outweighed by the losses it has experienced over the last several years. In general, the benefits from borrowing really have to be weighed against the cost. And the costs repeatedly appear to be much greater than people have fully taken into account.

Finally, let me say that underlying the policies in Argentina and many of the other reform strategies in Latin America have been these market fundamentalist ideas – the Washington consensus, which has argued for a minimalist role for government and very strongly against industrial policies. There is an alternative – a third way between the statist policies of the past and the market fundamentalist policies of the IMF. It is one that involves a more significant role for the government but also recognizes the importance of emerging forces.

It will be more difficult to craft such policies in today's era when there are restrictions imposed by WTO and other international agreements. Brazil, however, is beginning to show the way through more aggressive attitudes towards the United States, recognizing U.S. violations of those international agreements. There are creative ways to living within those international agreements.

The bottom line is that there are alternative strategies involving a commitment to objectives that are broader than those of the Washington consensus, of not only growth but also equality, democracy, and sustainable growth. They use a broader vision of economic processes; one recognizing that there is an important role for markets, but also an important role for government. The wisdom here is trying to get the appropriate balance between the two.

VI

Looking Ahead

12
Addressing
the Social Agenda

Michael Cohen

The discussion about the future of economic and social development in Argentina needs to be placed into a broader context. As we see the downward sloping lines on the graphs of economic performance, we have learned about the dynamics of recession and the growing impact on Argentina and increasing poverty in general. I think it is very important to raise the question of the distribution of income and the levels of inequality that existed within the country *prior* to the current crisis in order to frame the social agenda for the future.

I would like to move from the broader macro-economic level to a somewhat more micro-level view and connect my remarks to some of the other chapters of this volume. I believe that there are important connections that the macro-economists, frankly, do not always focus on. I make this observation based on having spent a number of years in the World Bank and having seen that these connections are not always made.

When I was living in Buenos Aires, one of the things that struck me almost every day was that the newspapers of Argentina express the view that economic well-being, *bienestar,* is related to employment, and employment creation itself depends on external forces. This observation is consistent with some of the earlier papers in this volume that commented about how people look outwards from Argentina, and particularly those who are from families of immigrants. It seemed to me that people seem to believe that what Mr. Soros did in the financial markets, the policies of Malaysia, the impact of the Asian financial crisis, or what the Russians or Brazilians were doing, all had a very strong impact on their own *bienestar.* This is somewhat curious, because, after all, when you are living in Buenos Aires, you see a large vibrant city, with many very intelligent people, a lot of exchange, activity, and creativity – all of which suggests that local decisions and initiative have significant impacts on daily life. So why was there so much looking outside? And did this behavior have anything to do with the predicament itself, with the problem of inequality and poverty?

As I drove around the city over several years, I could see enormous differences between the northeast corridors and the south of the city. I spent time in the periphery of Buenos Aires, in some of the slum areas, and the more I saw, the sense I drew was that there is a paradox: while there are great differences within Buenos Aires and indeed, within Argentina itself, these differences were not even recognized in the policy discussions.

At a meeting at the School of Architecture and Urban Planning of the University of Buenos Aires, I posed the question to a group of urban planners: "What is the second city of Argentina?" "It is obvious," many replied, "Córdoba is the second city." But Córdoba is not the second city of Argentina – La Matanza, which is a municipal area on the periphery of Buenos Aires with one and a half million people, 95% of whom are poor, is the second city. This community was not recognized either by the urbanists nor, most certainly, by the economists.

As I began to explore this question, I examined the distribution of public investment in Buenos Aires. I discovered that during the period 1990-97, the distribution of public funds for infrastructure – roads, electricity, water supply, public parks, traffic lights, and some social services – was highly skewed to richer areas of the city. Indeed, 68% of the investment in infrastructure went to neighborhoods that had 11.5% of the population.

I began to think about the distribution of public investment in light of the perception of external responsibility for local *bienestar*. I asked my friends in the city government of Buenos Aires, "Who is making these decisions? Are they coming from Washington or from Asia?" People said, "No, no, no, they are our decisions. We are following a set of resource allocation decisions involving infrastructure." This legacy of public decisions is a clear example that part of the intra-urban inequality of the 1990s is a result of local decisions and is therefore a local product.

This issue is relevant as we examine the indicators of the current recession in Argentina. We talk about those arrows going down, but it is clear that change is not equally felt at all income levels. Poor unemployed people are feeling the impact of contracting labor markets and increasing prices for staple goods more than middle and upper-income people. Similarly, as public expenditure contracts, for example for neighborhood infrastructure, those areas not already having adequate services will be further disadvantaged.

The conclusion of my study was that if I know your zip code in Buenos Aires, I can tell you who your children will be. The quality of health, education, environmental con-

ditions, infrastructure at the neighborhood level all corre-
late very closely with one another, as well as with crime.
These correlations between the lack of investment and
poor socio-economic conditions were rather robust and
convincing.

While the economic and social implications of this
analysis are striking, there is also an intriguing cultural
interpretation. When I discussed the conclusions with the
city government, national government, and academics,
their comment was, "There is nothing new here. We know
that investment is concentrated in some parts of the city
and other parts are ignored." Someone observed that
Borges had even mentioned this fact, writing that people
who lived north of Avenida Rivadavia in Buenos Aires were
rich, while those to its south were poor. This suggests that
intra-urban inequality is not just an economic fact or a
policy outcome, but also a cultural fact – what is visible
and what is invisible.

Now, in a time of crisis in which economic and social
conditions are deteriorating, maybe even at an increasing
rate, what is visible in Buenos Aires? What social and economic realities are identified as serious issues? This
reminds me of the debate in the early 1960s in the United
States when Michael Harrington wrote *The Other America,*
in which he argued that there was widespread poverty in
the country but that it was invisible to the average citizen
and the media. It proved to be a wake-up call and led to
the War on Poverty launched by the Johnson Administration
in the mid-1960s.

I would argue that the legacy of deep social and economic differences between categories of the Argentine
population must be recognized and addressed, as measures are developed to deal with the present economic crisis. It is an important item for the agenda of managing the
transition itself. It is not simply that the government must

stabilize the economy, but rather, to look and say, at this moment, how do we also deal with the legacy of the 1990s when inequality increased dramatically?

Here it seems that the agenda must connect to the agenda of investment. There must be some explicit recognition about the groups in the population that have suffered the most *before* the most recent crisis – i.e. as represented for example by the *piqueteros* – and who are also affected by the current crisis.

There is also an important analytical point, and this relates to the perception in the World Bank, the IMF, and conventional development economics about the significance of inequality. In 1998, the World Bank started a poverty assessment in Buenos Aires that was eventually published under the title *Poor People in a Rich Country*. In that piece of work, they looked at levels of poverty around Argentina and in Buenos Aires. At the time, I was working in the Bank, based in Buenos Aires, and I was in the middle of the study mentioned above. On the basis of the data on the distribution of public investment in infrastructure, I argued that the World Bank study needed to go beyond analyzing absolute poverty and should study inequality as well. I submitted the report that discussed the above, on the ecological basis of differences and the spatial distribution of investment. The Bank people answered that spatial distribution does not really contribute to inequality. Rather, the most important factors contributing to inequality are the returns on labor and education as reflected in wages.

Without disputing the importance of wages, I believe employment and wages are necessary but not sufficient conditions for targeting and identifying the poor in a large city like Buenos Aires. We know that many, many people in the city of Buenos Aires were relatively well off, were educated, and are now becoming poorer. At the same time, however, another six or seven million people on the periphery are desperately poor, lacking water, sanitation, food, and employment. The people living downtown are not the hungry – rather, the hungry are mostly those on the periphery under the current crisis. So we really need to think not simply in terms of macroeconomic aggregates, but rather in terms of the location of poverty distributed throughout the country and within urban areas. Maps of poverty and inequality for Buenos Aires will not be the same for Santo Fe, Córdoba, and other places. The Ministry of Social Development has reliable data on intra-urban distribution of infrastructure and social services.

This suggests that we also need to look at the real sector in this discussion, where investment might be targeted, and which areas in the city need attention. When we talk about a transition, we need not just a macroeconomic transition – we need a microeconomic and a spatial transition as well. This requires "place-specific" assessments and the recognition that some communities are more in trouble than others.

Targeting assistance to the most needy through spatial analysis allows the use of both an analytical category and a normative category. Neither disputes the importance of macroeconomic variables, but brings an added dimension to the translation of macro objectives into operational targets. It also helps to distinguish levels of intervention by implying that local institutions support the local level. This includes improving the consumption of social services, investment in infrastructure, and the use of labor intensive investments to generate jobs and contribute to economic growth. All of this can be initiated and supported by national and local agencies and need not rely on international assistance.

One of the comments made during the conference was, what would happen if there were no IMF or external institution to help in the current situation? What would Argentina do without assistance from outside? One of the arenas in which initiatives could begin today is the municipal level. Municipal infrastructure can serve as a bridge between investment and needed consumption of essential services. The country, after all, is largely urban, in both its population and the composition of its GDP.

Finally, thinking through the inter-sectoral connections is part of the agenda for this conference. If Argentina relies simply on macroeconomic analysis without translating its implications to local realities, it will face yet another set of obstacles. In political terms, these connections also serve as mechanisms of political accountability and feedback that are so needed in policy making in a democratic framework.

13

IN SEARCH OF THE (LOST) WORLD TO COME

MARGARITA GUTMAN

WHY DIDN'T ANYONE SAY ANYTHING?

Some of the many questions asked today in different forms about Argentina's dramatic situation are: "Why didn't anyone say anything? Why didn't anyone warn us about what could happen to us with continued convertibility and more neo-liberal policies? Why didn't anyone say "the emperor has no clothes!" These questions are always asked with the same bitterness.

It is not surprising that after the upheavals of December 2001, almost everybody is asking these same questions. Nor it is surprising that many specialists can answer these questions very well. In this volume, Halperín Donghi provides a clear historical explanation; Roberto Frenkel explains the situation through economic analysis; and Adriana Clemente interprets the impact of social policies.

However, it is not true that the storm arrived without warnings. Nor is it true that these explanations appeared

179

suddenly. On the contrary, there were warnings, commentaries, opinions, and criticisms in public and private debates and publications.[1] What was missing was a large receptive audience prepared to listen and repeat them, to articulate them in their own way, to accept or to argue, to support or reject. In fact, what was missing was the multiplication and amplification of these debates, spreading like an oil slick into each house, onto the kitchen table, in coffee bars, along the corridors of work places, in neighborhood plazas and clubs, in lecture halls, on television, radio, and other media.

This is what was missing before December 2001: an extended and intense public debate. Even if it would have been disorganized, heated, and difficult, the mere discussion of neo-liberal policies and their consequences – who gained, who lost, what were the risks, and who the victims – could have improved the possibility of seeing alternatives to the present situation.

The sudden appearance of people in the streets, seeing each other, fueled and energized the protest in public spaces of all the cities of the country.[2] This triggered not

---

[1] In chapter 10 of this volume, Joseph Stiglitz asks instead how it was that the social riots took so much time to explode. The perception of the "surprise factor" is also criticized in a recent book: "There is nothing more false than this idea of the sudden eruption: There is nothing that has happened in Argentina that is not prepared for months, years: in order to see it it was necessary just to want to see it. And many did not want to." (Martín Caparrós. Qué País, Planeta, Buenos Aires, 2002, page 17). The critiques that were made against the privatization process during the 1990s are accurately analyzed by Daniel Cecchini and Jorge Zicolillo in Los Nuevos Conquistadores, Foca, Madrid, 2002. The last 25 years in Argentina are analyzed by Carlos Gabetta in La Debacle de Argentina, Icaria. Barcelona, 2002, which argues there were deliberate corruption and misleading statements – a merciless swindle carried out by officials in charge of public policies.

[2] 13,000 protests occurred from January to September 2002.

only the fall of the government but an enormous wave of public discussion which has continued for months. At the end of many years of apparent acceptance – with resignation or indifference – suddenly the doors of communication between people opened in the same way that occurred with other tragedies and disasters elsewhere. But more than anything, in December 2001, the events released the capacity of Argentines to ask themselves out loud: "For whom are we playing the neo-liberal game?" Together with the pain and the rage provoked by the critical situation in which the people now find themselves, the paths were opened towards a collective rethinking that offers at least the possibility of discussing alternatives for the short and medium term, including their implementation.[3]

In sum, this public discussion is leading to nothing less than a collective recovery of thinking about the future. Thinking about the future is a cornerstone of the identity of any social group of whatever size – whether local, regional, or national – no matter how close the group is to the winds of globalization.

Only a Crisis?

In the first months of 2002, in villages and big cities, in the streets and in the media, people talked, with regret and

---

[3] For the description of the crisis as a fruitful field for positive transformations, see the mentioned book by Caparrós, where this analysis is made and a wide range of personalities, such as Jorge Lanata, Víctor De Gennaro, Claudio Lozano, Elisa Carrió, Luis D'Elia, Luis Bilbao, Horacio González and Julio Nudler, among others, are interviewed.

anger, about collapse, bankruptcy, economic and social crisis, deep crisis, and final crisis. President Duhalde himself, in his inaugural speech of January 1, 2002, said "we are bankrupt." Thus, as "crisis" and "collapse," this is the way people are describing the process that we are living in in Argentina today and apparently it is accepted as such.

But this process is more than six months long if we count only from December 2001 when the evidence of the disaster was visible to everyone and not only to those who suffered the most or who were taking advantage of the situation. Can it be described as a crisis if it is only the tip of an iceberg which has been growing since the mid-1970s? [4]

If this were only a crisis, it would have not lasted so long. The condition of being extended in time is almost a contradiction with the meaning of crisis itself. A crisis hits and passes, allowing a quick reaction – toward success or failure – but in the end always leads to a break, a time to recover one's breath. That is not the case of Argentina today. Today there is no possible space to relax and to breathe.

Why is this so? Because Argentina has been astonished for a long time by the collapse of its foundational myths: of being a rich country, of being the breadbasket of the world, and of being on an ascendant and continuous path of progress and improvement. Because it has also for

---

[4] As explained in this volume by various authors, the problems derived from the neo-liberal model and from how the local agents adopted it – far from a concern about the public interest and only addressed to maintaining the dominant groups in power. This became clearly visible during the 1990s, but its foundations can be seen in the 1970s, when the military regime, the "Proceso," applied the neo-liberal model right after starting State Terrorism.

years been feeling the silent pain of real and imaginary losses, but more than anything, because it feels the pain of the lost right to work and to have access to a minimum wage allowing a life with dignity. Because a people continually impoverished over the last 25 years are suffering deeply, with resignation. And because hunger is now present in our streets – a hunger that we naively believed, as children, was only suffered by distant relatives who survived in post-war Europe or by exotic inhabitants of Africa and Asia[5].

The continuation of this process of collective suffering, coupled with a wider discussion shown in part by the *piquetes, cacerolazos* and neighborhood assemblies, allows us to think that perhaps what is happening is not just another crisis. Nor is it an ending, but rather a true transformation. The nature of this process may be prompting a deep change in the society and its culture. Whether it will have a good or bad ending is another question, which depends on what will be done by Argentines and the international community. This process depends on both, but it can only be managed and led by Argentines.

In this way, the passing of time, while painful, allows at least the possibility of a change in social and cultural practices. These changes require time as an input; they have to be lived and experienced in the medium and long term, acknowledging the past while planning for the future. These changes, in ideas, perceptions of oneself and of others, behaviors and routines, modes of expression and communication, all require time to be achieved.

---

5 *Dolor país (Country Pain)* – as opposed to the ill-renowned "country risk" – is the title given by psychologist Silvia Bleichmar to a small volume that gathers articles published in 2001. (Buenos Aires, Libros del Zorzal).

This is to say, that besides effective social and economic policies, time is necessary to try out solutions, to make mistakes, to create by doing, to reflect, and to try again, individually and collectively.

There is a biological image that can illustrate this process: it is known that nervous connections in the brain are a complex web that, in order to register a change from a state 1 to a state 2, have to have register changes in each of their countless nodes. Only when all the nodes have produced a re-connection, when all those many small changes have been produced, can the system pass from one state to the other. To perceive a change, even the smallest one, the transformation should be experienced by each one of the countless nodes that constitute social, cultural, political and economic relations. Neither executive orders nor social or economic policies can produce a change from one day to the next in cultural practices.

In this way, it is possible that the task of transformation, which we can define as cultural and social reconstruction, is *"total y prolongada"*. Perhaps, along with the statement *"Nunca Más"* (Never Again) to the 1976 military dictatorship, we should say never again to the belief that is possible to find shortcuts, exits and quick solutions, charismatic, magic, and easy. I would dare to suggest that, more than laying out critiques and projects, one of our challenges today is to find the direction of change to orient the small steps and transformations leading to the reconstruction of a viable future. Small steps, well oriented, are more effective that all-or-nothing, black or white solutions. Moreover, through those millions of small steps, it will perhaps be possible to dismantle the impunity that – far from any worry about the public good – covered the sale of the national assets of the country.

The Gates of Hell[6]

It is true that the massive public takeover of streets and roads in our country is not new as a visible and spatial expression of collective protest. But there is a new aspect of these protests, recognized by many, which is definitely threatening. It is the absence of any hope, the divestiture of the future.

This absence of a future is heard in different kinds of comments on the streets, many of which have been recorded by Silvio Fishbein in his video "¡Basta!" (Stop!) In this volume, García Canclini analyzes these issues as they appear in literature and street life. It has also been commented on by the media. This absence of a future is evident in everyday discussions on any streetcorner of the city: Are you staying or leaving? Where are you going? How? What will you do? "To leave" as a slogan, coupled with the anxiety filling the lines of people in front of the embassies, is simply one more expression of the abandonment by the middle class of the idea of a possible future in the country. If they stay, young people are those who have more to lose.

The absence of a future is not news for the poor; they have always lived on a day-to-day basis and have always had their future confiscated by the system. The rich can afford the luxury of playing with the punk idea of "no future" – as Caparrós points out. But for the once large Argentine middle class, who believed up to last year that they belonged to the gilded circle of the first world, this

---

6 "Per me si va ne la città dolente/ per me si va ne l'eterno dolore,/ per me si va tra la perduta gente (...) lasciate ogni speranza, voi ch'entrate" (Dante).

total confiscation of a future is an almost mortal blow[7]. In fact, it is an unbearable discovery for a society that, over the last one hundred years, has lived convinced of a future of unlimited progress, with an automatically updated insurance policy based in the productivity of the land and the educational level of its inhabitants. There is no doubt that this loss of the future is one of the more harrowing consequences of these last 25 years. For this reason, the revival of public discussion about the future is one of the most urgent challenges for the transformation that lies ahead.

THE FUTURE FOR WHAT?

There is a vast reflection on the future produced by philosophers, essayists, and writers through utopias, science fiction, and other genres which talk about the future in more or less explicit ways[8]. I will only quote Paul Ricoeur, who analyzes the tension between ideology and utopia, which he defines as basic components of social

---

[7] The confiscation of the future can be found in many reflections in the articles by Susana Torrado and Martín Caparrós published in *Qué País*, as well as in the book by Silvia Bleichmar.

[8] The two words from which 'utopia' come are 'ou' and 'topos,' that refer to 'non-places,' which is to say, that an utopia can be in some other space, or in another time in the future. Other interpretations are derived from the words 'eu' and 'topos,' designating a 'good place.' Based in this ambiguity — present also in utopian thought since Thomas More wrote his celebrated work in 1515-1516 — it is possible to consider utopia as one of the manifestations of thought about the future.

imagination[9]. Ricoeur understands utopia as the inseparable part of collective imagination, linked and opposed to — but always interacting with — ideology. This is to say that every society needs both components in continuous interaction in order to function correctly and develop. When one of them disappears from the horizon of the imaginary — either as cause or effect of historical circumstances — it produces a deep imbalance in society or in individuals.

Ricoeur highlights the essentially conflictive structure of this double imaginary, where each of these concepts has a positive and negative aspect. This is to say that ideology as well as utopia have both constructive and destructive functions. But the negative side is what first appears on the surface in each case. For example: by *ideology*, we can understand a process of distortions and disguise through which certain situations are hidden. In this way ideology is associated with social untruth or, even worse, ideology is associated with a protective illusion of a social status, with all the privileges and injustices that this implies. At the same time, utopia is accused of not being more than an escape from reality, "a sort of science fiction applied to politics." Utopian projects are discarded for their geometry and rigidity, and because they lack a logic of action. In this way, utopia would not be more than a way of "dreaming of action while avoiding reflecting on the conditions for the possibility of insertion in the current situation[10]."

However, when analyzing, in depth, the three levels where both utopia and ideology are expressed, Ricoeur

---

[9] Paul Ricoeur, "La ideología y la utopía: dos expresiones del imaginario social," in *Del texto a la acción*, Fondo de Cultura Económica, Buenos Aires, 2002.
[10] Ricoeur, 2002, p. 350.

highlights the powerful, positive, and constructive function that both elements have. In the case of ideology, on the first level – the most shallow and pejorative – it is understood as distortion or disguise. On a second level, Ricoeur identifies the function of ideology as that of legitimizing power, used more to justify than to falsify, and directly linked to the phenomenon of domination. "No society works without norms, rules and a whole social symbolism that, in turn, requires a rhetoric of public discourse.[11]" According to Ricoeur, this rhetoric of public discourse becomes ideology when it legitimates power. Finally, on the third and most fundamental level, ideology works as an element of integration of the community. It does so on a deeper level than that of legitimation (in relation to power) and, of course, than the superficial level of disguise. Ideology, on its constructive and positive level, works then as a "bond with the collective memory" in order to transform the founding events into beliefs of the whole community. Any group "represents its existence through an idea, an idealized image of itself, and that image reinforces its identity[12]."

In the same way that ideology preserves reality, utopia questions it. In this way, utopia is the expression of all the potentialities of any group that are repressed by the ruling order. At its deepest level, utopia is radically opposed to the integrative function of ideology. On this third level, in the opposite extreme of the shallow and cartoon level of fantasies of escape, utopias have the power of pushing people to question reality, of going further than what is immediately visible or is obscured by the ruling order.

At an intermediate level, utopia is radically opposed to the legitimizing function of ideology. And on the most

---

[11] Ricoeur, 2002, p. 353.
[12] Ricoeur, 2002,. p. 356.

superficial level, by skipping any practical or political reflection (and as the escapist and frenetic fantasy of what is all-or-nothing, immediately obtained), utopia can push us "to jump forward senselessly toward another place, with all the risks of a mad and even bloody discourse.[13]"

Beyond the variety of forms adopted by utopias that by definition are as multiple and diverse as the efforts of the imagination to think of another way of life, Ricoeur points out that utopia's function is more important than its content. The common basis of the most diverse forms of utopia is not the content, but the subversive function in relation to the current social order. It is subversive because it opens another way of thinking and doing.

In this way, Ricoeur shows that, at its deepest level, utopia allows the expression of social and individual potentialities. This positive and constructive aspect of utopia is a potential and powerful tool that societies can use to change themselves. In this manner, utopia has a wholly liberating function that helps to understand the possibilities of an alternative society and an alternative city.

IN SEARCH OF THE (LOST) WORLD TO COME

If we think about what happened in Argentina during the last ten years, it would seem that ideology — as a discourse that legitimates the neo-liberal model — completely covered the horizon of the social imaginary. The question that

---

[13] Ricoeur, 2002, p. 359.

opens this chapter of the book – "Why didn't anybody say anything?" – can be understood, in Ricoeur's terms, as an expression of the ideological weight that the neo-liberal model and convertibility had over the social imagination. A foreign observer forecast: "Argentina: victim of ideology.[14]" Legitimizing "the model" worked to perpetuate it through a well-designed discourse. The deaf void into which all the warnings and predictions fell, reveals the absence of almost all constructive utopian thought, which would have been a fertile field where possible alternatives could have been produced.

Through this volume it is possible to see how there has been a growing gap between the people who have more and those who have less. This has been explained from economic, historical, social, and cultural perspectives. This gap represents the increasing social injustice and inequality that began around 1975, although according to many studies it started even before. At the same time, in a parallel process, but in the other direction, utopian thought was disappearing, which smothered not only thoughts about the future, but along with it, the possibility of thinking of alternatives.

The public debate generated since the December 2001 events can be an arena for the development of deeper and more constructive utopian thought. The absence of hope or of a collective project for the future simply undermines a society's capacity to react and change.

In fact, it is sad to observe that this opening to thinking about new alternatives, the collective reflection that

---

[14] Paul Krugman, "A cross of dollars," *The New York Times*, November 7, 2001, p. 23.

was smothered and denied for years, was triggered by the dramatic outcome of December 2001. However, in spite of the drama, the current situation is without doubt a great opportunity. Maybe we will now be more conscious of the necessity of defending this capacity for collective reflection that feeds the more creative and positive part of utopian thought.

Another of the challenges in front of us is not to lose the opportunity created by these dramatic events. Whatever happens, the only inalienable right that still stands is the right to exert reflective thought. Exercising this right is a tool to defend ourselves against fraudulent attacks on public liberty. But it also encourages the collective construction of a project for the future.

POSTSCRIPT.
TRAGEDIES AND COLLAPSES:
COLLATERAL EFFECTS

For the first time in my life, I happen to live far from our country during a time of conflict. I followed the events of December 2001 by the minute, from another city recently attacked in an almost inconceivable way: New York. Monthly trips to Buenos Aires threw me into two serious crises at the same time. I went from the crowds filling the streets of New York in a silent search for missing loved ones and friends, to the noisy streets and plazas of Buenos Aires, crowded with people clanging pots and pans and with the clamor of pickets protesting the lack of jobs.

In spite of the different circumstances and facts that triggered the tragedies, in each of these cities I could see strength unfold after a tragedy – after a collapse – that threw people into the streets and opened channels of communication. In both cities, even in the middle of the paralysis produced by pain, shock, and bitterness, an intense and participatory public discussion emerged about what to do in the short and long run. In New York, discussions quickly went from the future of Ground Zero to the future of Lower Manhattan, and even, for some, to the future of the city as a whole.

In both cities, with apparently different problems, tragedy triggered similar debates whirling around the future of each society. It is not possible to know how each case will unfold, but we do know as a certainty that public discussion about the future is an irreversible fact: without it, there is no chance at all to build a future for all.

EPILOGUE

NEOLIBERALISM AND ARGENTINA

JEFFREY MADRICK

Everyone talked about America's electronics and enter-
tainment exports in the 1990s, but the nation's proudest
and most influential export may have been neoliberal economics. Argentina was also neoliberalism's most enthusi-
astic importer. The reasons for this form a complex and
confounding question. Even doctrinaire Chile adopted
serious regulations to limit capital flows. But it was fairly
clear, except to the enthusiasts, that Argentina's extreme
adoption of neoliberal ideology, especially the pegging of
its currency to the dollar, was bound to fail. The relevant
characteristics of America's neoliberal economics were the
free flow of capital, goods and services; restrained government spending; a stable currency; low inflation; limited
regulation; and moderate debt.

The word neoliberalism confuses people these days. It
is interesting that this nineteenth century description of
what is basically laissez-faire economics has caught on in
recent years. It harkens back to the original meaning of

liberalism in the eighteenth and nineteenth centuries. Then, the world's fledgling democracies were "liberating" their people from the tyranny of monarchies and feudal aristocracies. Adam Smith's *Wealth of Nations* was a moral argument for the power and rights of the individual, which in turn would ensure the common good.

Towards the end of the nineteenth century, liberalism came to mean something different. It was broadly accepted that government was now necessary to liberate and protect people from the rising power of industry and new oligarchic interests, rather than the other way around. The United States' progressive age began more or less with Theodore Roosevelt and involved the aggressive use of government to regulate business and finance; protect individuals, workers and investors; and invest in public goods that industry neglected. To call laissez-faire economics neoliberalism, then, is a stretch of recent history, but one that fits the purpose. It sounds liberating, but from whom? The culprit is again big government, which, advocates claim, is inefficient, bumbling, unaffordable, and often corrupt.

The movement back towards laissez-faire economics and neoliberalism in general began in the 1970s and was led by the United States. This in itself is why it gained so much authority around the world. It is important to realize that it was "reborn" in the uncertainty, and most importantly, newly straitened economic conditions of the 1970s in the U.S. High inflation and high unemployment confused and angered Americans. Male wages stagnated. Spouses rushed to work, but family income hardly rose after inflation on average. High interest rates made it difficult to buy a house. Soaring education and healthcare costs pushed many out of the middle class. Even as inflation came down in the 1980s, the rate of economic growth did not improve. Wages remained low, family incomes grew slowly, and government abandoned its customary role to create new institutions, such as public daycare, to help in changing times. The nation sought an explanation for its discontent, and the answer was big government, which was seen as unpredictable. Progressivism, or twentieth century liberalism, in which government was used affirmatively, had run its course.

A number of factors contributed to making government the principal culprit. One was moral exhaustion after the Vietnam War, which after all was led by 1960s liberals and advocates of government intervention. It was analogous to the moral exhaustion after the Civil War, which led to the era of Social Darwinism. There was also moral exhaustion over the intense social battles of the 1960s, which involved inner city rioting, hippie revolution, and rising antagonism towards business. The wars on prejudice and poverty that resulted were more successful than is realized in retrospect, but they were enervating.

Another reason nations often choose a particular direction is simply because it is different or even the opposite of the course they previously followed. Except for historical moments in the 1920s and 1950s, Americans had adopted modest progressivism as their central political philosophy for seventy years. The progressive movement also went too far in several respects. It respected business and the markets too little and took too little time in devising efficient and far-seeing government programs. The war on poverty in the U.S. was a success in many ways but not in all respects. Backlash is never inevitable but it was likely, and in some respects, necessary.

There are two final reasons for the rise of neoliberalism. One is that neoliberalism was profitable to the privileged and powerful in the United States, and especially those in the new elite services, including finance, marketing, and management. The final reason is the most important because it may tell us the most about the world's future. Neoliberalism coincided best with America's national character. It retreated to old-fashioned notions about self-reliance and individualism. America never had a cozy relationship with government. Its freedom was founded in escaping from government and its character is deeply based in its fear of the government.

Progressivism took root and gained momentum only in a time of extraordinary prosperity. The American people could easily afford the higher taxes needed for social programs, regulation, and the role of watchdog. The New Deal was a product of the Great Depression, but the progressive movement still had a great deal of momentum from the Roosevelt-Wilson years. That momentum would carry right through until the 1960s, another period of high prosperity. Yet in the 1970s, that all changed. There was no budgetary room in the typical family for taxes and little emotional room for compassion for others. More than anything else, it was straitened economic conditions that hastened the second coming of old-fashioned antigovernment neo-liberalism in the United States.

American financial power, and its influence over the World Bank and the International Monetary Fund, of course, is what gave neoliberal economics weight in the rest of the world. Yet Argentina adopted the economic strategy long before it could be called a success and when few talked about a "new economy." The American boom was not the proof Argentina required to go headlong in the direction of neoliberalism.

Because faith in these policies continues more or less unabated, it is relevant to discuss whether neoliberalism is what caused the U.S. boom in the late 1990s. The new laissez-faire attitude took deep root under Ronald Reagan in the early 1980s long before the economic boom. The centerpiece of the new policy was the record-setting tax cut he sponsored, which ultimately reduced income tax rates and corporate taxes in particular by large amounts. Reagan also embarked on a policy of deregulation and privatization, reduced social spending by government, and an eloquent if historically simplistic call for a return to a nostalgic, comforting America – "it is morning again in America." Under Paul Volcker, the U.S. Federal Reserve made the fight against inflation its main battle, keeping interest rates high.

The results were hardly the sort the IMF would have approved. The U.S. federal budget and trade deficits soared and national savings fell. The economy grew, but productivity did not return to former rates of improvement. Meantime, the financial markets exploded and old-line industries shaved workers at a record pace under pressure from corporate raiders and stock market analysts. Incomes consistently grew unequal and wages for males continued to fall on average, characteristics consistent with the practice of neoliberal economics around the world. The U.S. economic boom did not occur until late 1995, thirteen or fourteen years after the Reagan tax cuts and sixteen or so years after the fight against inflation had begun in earnest. Promises of rising capital investment went unfulfilled in the 1980s and even early 1990s. Savings increasingly fell, instead of growing.

Given this history, it is hard – in fact, wrong – to make a case that neoliberal economics accounted for the U.S. takeoff. Other, more conventional factors, and the exponential effect of their impacts on one another, explain the event. A series of new standardized electronic products swept the market, from Windows to Cisco to AOL, generating enormous economies of scale (including in retailing – the Wal-Mart effect.) Computer chip prices virtually collapsed in the 1990s, making high technology investment cheaper. The rising stock market and housing market supported enormous increases in consumer spending as individuals borrowed freely. The dollar remained high despite the rising trade deficit.

Neoliberal economies mat have had some part, we must acknowledge, but not a large part. In the 2000s, the U.S. faces serious obstacles to its economic future: high levels of debt, a falling stock market, and over-investment in general. Hundreds of billions of dollars were invested based on poor signals from its absurdly overvalued stock market. Yet the power of neoliberal economics over the world remains almost undiminished.

I have two questions to ask Argentina. First, why peg the peso to the dollar at a one-to-one rate when the U.S. is influenced by economic factors that do not influence Argentina? The partial answer is that pegging to the dollar is nothing more than a disciplinary device that forces monetary authorities to restrain themselves from pumping up the money supply. Yet when the dollar rose to unimaginable heights in the late 1990s, it did so for reasons that had no analogue in Argentina and it put the latter nation at a terrible disadvantage with regard to its trading partners. Argentina should have enough confidence to guide its own fate. The dollar peg, ironically, demonstrated the low level of confidence within the nation.

Second, why peg the peso to the dollar when the U.S., the great exporter of neoliberal economics, does not have to play by the same disciplinary rules? Now that the U.S. economy has weakened, it turns to its federal budget deficits without pause for reflection. Argentina could not do that – the IMF would not let it. The U.S. urges its central bank to lower interest rates with little concern for inflation. Argentina could not have done that. The U.S. ignored a growing trade deficit for years. Other nations, including Argentina, cannot do that. America enjoys the best of both worlds. It suffers little pain compared to other nations that adopt the same policies. No other nation has the might or the reserve currency to do that.

The deep error – in truth, it was a deep hole – on the part of Argentina was faith in universal answers. Economics, despite the preaching of many trained and often seemingly glamorous economists, does not offer universal solutions. It provides tools to deal with current situations, not a set of policies appropriate to all circumstances – the world is not that easy. Those who believe a currency can be pegged to a simple value and held there indefinitely do not deal with the realities of this world.

Neoliberal economics may soon even hurt the U.S. It has bred a callous attitude towards the nation's poor, growing inequality in general, inadequate healthcare, and, in particular, blindness to the plight of children. It has also tolerated and rationalized absurd speculative excess in the name of laissez-faire philosophies and deregulation.

Most damaging, neoliberal economics has disoriented the U.S., and all nations it influences, about the true causes of growth. Savings and capital flows and free trade are important. At least equally as important, is the strength and vitality of a nation's domestic market; history argues strongly that the strength of such markets matter more. Inequality of incomes undermines such a market; disadvantages in education and opportunity for large pockets of a population also hurt this market; stagnating wages hurt this market; and inadequate transportation limits demand. A glaring outcome of the reigning economic philosophy is its benefits to those with money and power more than to those who merely work for a living.

We who believe neoliberal economics went too far should not make the equal and opposite mistake, however. We should recognize what is valuable in neoliberal economics. Markets are extraordinary creations: the flow of capital is useful and freer trade is generally desirable. There is occasionally room for import substitution, and even tariffs to protect certain industries. Government policies should be within reason, not simple expediencies to solve momentary political discontent. Even these are not answers in themselves, certainly not universal answers. Moreover, I do not have a prescription for fighting the prevailing conventional wisdom, so forcefully enforced by the International Monetary Fund and the now-famed "Washington consensus."

I would urge other nations to think for themselves. If they must make compromises with powerful financial forces, then at least they should not become victim to the glamour of wealth in the North. The exotic often has undeserved appeal, but the U.S. has not solved all or perhaps even its most central economic problems – be wary of it as a model. Accept what is good but firmly reject what is either bad of inappropriate. Latin America's future lies within itself, not in looking to the North. The domestic political obstacles to economic union and common policies are beyond my scope, but I would urge the continent to look to its own strength and trust its own instincts. There is no special answer in the answer in the North and certainly not one free of the bias of its own interests.

ANNEX

Conference Participants and Program

Economic Management and Political Collapse in Argentina: Interpreting the Past to Build for the Future

April 8-9, 2002

April 8

Opening

Screening of *Basta!: Argentina in Crisis*, a video by Silvio Fischbein, University of Buenos Aires.

Welcome
- Bob Kerrey, President, New School University.
- Michael Cohen, Director, Graduate Program in International Affairs, The New School.

SESSION I

INTRODUCTION

• Jorge Balán, The Ford Foundation.

ARGENTINA IN HISTORICAL PERSPECTIVE: WHY DID ARGENTINA ADOPT A NEO-LIBERAL MODEL?

• Tulio Halperín Donghi, Professor of History, University of California, Berkeley.

SESSION II

THE MODEL IN PRACTICE: COSTS AND BENEFITS – A ROUNDTABLE

CHAIR:
• Jeffrey Madrick, Economics Writer, *The New York Times.*

PANELISTS:
• Roberto Frenkel, Director, Bank of the Province of Buenos Aires.
• José Marcio Camargo, Pontifical Catholic University, Brazil.
• Andrés Solimano, UN Economic Commission for Latin America and the Caribbean.

SESSION III
IMPACTS OF THE CRISIS

CHAIR:
• Caroline Moser, Adjunct Professor, Graduate Program in International Affairs, New School; Senior Fellow, World Policy Institute.

PANELISTS:
• Berardo Dujovne, Dean, School of Architecture, Design, and Urban Planning, University of Buenos Aires, "The City of Buenos Aires".
• Adriana Clemente, Director, Social Policy and Poverty Program, International Institute for Environment and Development, "Social Impacts of the Crisis".

SESSION IV
POLITICAL ISSUES OF THE TRANSITION

CHAIR:
• Michael Cohen, Director, Graduate Program in International Affairs.

PANELISTS:
• Torcuato di Tella, Professor of Political Science, University of Buenos Aires.
• Victoria Murillo, Professor of Political Science, Yale University.
• Ernesto Semán, *Clarín*, Buenos Aires.

APRIL 9

SESSION V
POLICY ISSUES OF THE TRANSITION: FROM CRISIS TOWARDS SUSTAINABLE AND EQUITABLE GROWTH

CHAIR:
• Jeffrey Madrick, Economics Writer, *The New York Times.*

PANELISTS:
• Nicolás Dujovne, Chief Economist, Bank of Galicia, Buenos Aires, (former Chief Economic Advisor, Central Bank of Argentina), "Solving the Banking Crisis".
• Roberto Frenkel, Bank of the Province of Buenos Aires.
• Michael Cohen, Director, Graduate Program in International Affairs, The New School, "Inequality and the Social Agenda".

SESSION VI
NEW SPACES OF EXPRESSION

CHAIR:
• Margarita Gutman, Senior Fellow, Vera List Center for Art and Politics, The New School; School of Architecture, Design, and Urban Planning, University of Buenos Aires.

PANELISTS:
• Néstor García Canclini, Metropolitan Autonomous University-Iztapalapa, Mexico.
• Adhemar Bianchi, Director of the Catalinas Sur Theater group, Buenos Aires.

SESSION VII
INTERNATIONAL, REGIONAL AND NATIONAL RESPONSIBILITIES

CHAIR:
• Augusto Varas, The Ford Foundation.

PANELISTS:
• Joseph Tulchin, Woodrow Wilson International Center for Scholars.
• Diana Tussie, Professor, International Economic Relations, FLACSO, Buenos Aires.
• Andrés Solimano, UN Economic Commission for Latin America and the Caribbean.

SESSION VIII
CONCLUSION: PUTTING ARGENTINA IN PERSPECTIVE: TOWARDS CHANGING THE MODEL IN LATIN AMERICA

CHAIR:
• Michael Cohen, Director, Graduate Program in International Affairs.

SPEAKER:
• Joseph Stiglitz, Professor of Economics, Columbia University.

DISCUSSANTS:
• Tulio Halperín Donghi, Professor of History, University of California, Berkeley.

- Roberto Frenkel, Bank of the Province of Buenos Aires.
- Lance Taylor, Director, Center for Economic Policy Analysis, Arnhold Professor of International Cooperation and Development, Graduate Faculty, New School University.

LIST OF AUTHORS

JOSÉ MARCIO CAMARGO. Professor of Economics, Pontifical Catholic University, Rio de Janeiro.

ADRIANA CLEMENTE. Director, Social Policy and Poverty Program, International Institute for Environment and Development, IIED-Latin America; Director of Social Work Courses, University of Buenos Aires.

MICHAEL COHEN. Economist; Director, Graduate Program in International Affairs, The New School; President, International Institute for Environment and Development, IIED-Latin America; former Senior Advisor, and Chief, Urban Development Division, World Bank.

BERARDO DUJOVNE. Vice-Rector, University of Buenos Aires; Dean, School of Architecture, Design and Urban Planning, University of Buenos Aires.

NICOLÁS DUJOVNE. Chief Economist, Bank of Galicia, Buenos Aires.

ROBERTO FRENKEL. Director, Bank of the Province of Buenos Aires; Professor of Economics, University of Buenos Aires.

NÉSTOR GARCÍA CANCLINI. Metropolitan Autonomous University-Iztapalapa, Mexico.

MARGARITA GUTMAN. Senior Fellow, Vera List Center for Art and Politics, The New School; School of Architecture, Design, and Urban Planning, University of Buenos Aires; International Institute for Environment and Development, IIED-Latin America.

TULIO HALPERÍN DONGHI. Professor Emeritus of History, University of California at Berkeley.

JEFFREY MADRICK. Economics Writer, *The New York Times*; Senior Fellow, World Policy Institute.

ERNESTO SEMÁN. Journalist, *Clarín*, Buenos Aires.

ANDRÉS SOLIMANO. UN Economic Commission for Latin America and the Caribbean.

JOSEPH STIGLITZ. Nobel Laureate in Economics; Professor of Economics, Columbia University; former Chief Economist and Vice President, World Bank.

JOSEPH S. TULCHIN. Director, Latin American Studies Program, Woodrow Wilson International Center for Scholars, Washington, D.C.